**THE POLITICS OF NONVIOLENT ACTION** is a major exploration of the nature of nonviolent struggle. This unabridged edition is in three volumes: **Power and Struggle, The Methods of Nonviolent Action,** and **The Dynamics of Nonviolent Action.**

**Power and Struggle** begins with an examination of political power. It is often assumed that power derives from violence and can be controlled only by greater violence. Actually, power derives from sources in the society which may be restricted or severed by withdrawal of cooperation by the populace.

The political power of governments may in fact be very fragile. Even the power of dictators may be destroyed by withdrawal of the human assistance which made the regime possible.

Nonviolent action is based on that insight.

Basic characteristics of nonviolent struggle are described, misconceptions about it are corrected, and part of its vast history sketched. This has been action by ordinary people, not pacifists or saints, struggling imperfectly for their diverse causes.

Using nonviolent action, people have won higher wages, broken social barriers, changed government policies, frustrated invaders, paralyzed an empire and dissolved dictatorships.

**The Methods of Nonviolent Action** examines in detail 198 specific methods of this technique—broadly classed as nonviolent protest and persuasion, noncooperation (social, economic and political) and nonviolent intervention.

Each of these specific "nonviolent weapons" is illustrated with actual cases.

**The Dynamics of Nonviolent Action** examines the complex operation of this technique against a violent, repressive opponent.

Groundwork which may precede the struggle is explored, as well as basic requirements for effectives. Then the focus turns to the initial impact of the nonviolent challenge.

Repression is probable. Determined, yet nonviolent, continued resistance is needed to fight it. The opponent's repression may rebound by "political *jiu-jitsu,*" weakening his power by loss of support and increased resistance.

Three main mechanisms by which nonviolent action may produce victory are examined: conversion (the rarest), accommodation, and nonviolent coercion. Massive noncooperation may paralyze and disintegrate even an oppressive system.

All these elements of the dynamics of nonviolent struggle are illustrated with examples.

The resisting group itself is also changed: it gains in self-respect, confidence and power.

Empowerment of the struggle group, the accompanying strengthening of the non-State institutions, ability to defeat repressive elites, and the extension among the populace of a nonviolent struggle capacity, contribute to long-term social changes by redistributing power.

# Power
# and Struggle
## part one of:

Extending Horizons Books

A study prepared
under the auspices of
Harvard University's Center
for International Affairs

# The Politics of
# Nonviolent Action

## Gene Sharp

With the editorial assistance of Marina Finkelstein

*Porter Sargent Publishers, II Beacon St., Boston, Ma. 02108*

Library of Congress Catalog Number 72-95483
ISBN 0-87558-070-X

Eighth Printing, 2000


Illustrations by Robert Reitherman
Book Design by Sandi Mandeville Tatman
Production Coordinator of Original Edition: Jan Boddie

# GENE SHARP
## *A Biographical Profile*

Gene Sharp is Senior Scholar at the Albert Einstein Institution in Boston, Massachusetts. From 1965 he held research appointments in Harvard University's Center for International Affairs for nearly thirty years. He is Professor Emeritus of Political Science at the University of Massachusetts at Dartmouth.

Dr. Sharp, who has been called "the Clausewitz of nonviolent warfare," founded the Albert Einstein Institution in 1983 to promote research, policy studies, and education on the strategic uses of nonviolent struggle in face of dictatorship, war, genocide, and oppression.

He holds the degree of Doctor of Philosophy in Political Theory from Oxford University (1968), a Master of Arts in Sociology (1951), and a Bachelor of Arts in Social Sciences (1949) from Ohio State University. Manhattan College awarded him an honorary degree of Doctor of Laws (1983). Rivier College awarded him an honorary Doctor of Humanitarian Service (1996).

He lived for ten years in England and Norway. He did advanced studies at Oxford University, and in Norway he held positions at the University of Oslo and the Institute for Social Research.

Dr. Sharp is the author of various books on nonviolent struggle, power, political problems, dictatorships, and defense policy. His writings have been published in English in several countries and in twenty-seven other languages. These include Norwegian, German, French, Italian, Arabic, Hebrew, Tamil, Burmese, Karen, Thai, Spanish, Chinese, Korean, and Japanese.

His *The Politics of Nonviolent Action* (1973) (Introduction by Thomas C. Schelling) was immediately hailed as a classic and the definitive study of nonviolent struggle.

His *Making Europe Unconquerable* (1985) focused on the relevance of civilian-based defense for Western Europe. It carried a Foreword by George F. Kennan.

His *Civilian-Based Defense: A Post-Military Weapons System* (1990) examined how organized nonviolent noncooperation and defiance can potentially deter and defeat internal takeovers and invasions. This book was used in 1991 and 1992 by the new independent governments of Estonia, Latvia, and Lithuania in planning their defense against Soviet efforts to regain control.

A collection of political analyses, *Social Power and Political Freedom* (1980), included an Introduction by Senator Mark O. Hatfield.

*Gandhi as a Political Strategist, with Essays on Ethics and Politics* (1979) carried an Introduction by Coretta Scott King, and the Indian edition (1999) contained additionally a Foreword by Frederico Mayor, then Director-General of UNESCO.

His first book, *Gandhi Wields the Weapon of Moral Power* (1960) included a Foreword by Albert Einstein.

Additionally, he is co-editor of *Resistance, Politics, and the American Struggle for Independence, 1765-1775* (1986) and of *Nonviolent Action: A Research Guide* (1997), as well as a contributor to several encyclopedias.

A new book, *The Power and Practice of Nonviolent Struggle,* is in preparation in English. The earlier edition in Tibetan is being published with a Foreword by the Dalai Lama.

Dr. Sharp's recent shorter writings include *From Dictatorship to Democracy* (English, Burmese, Spanish, Karen, and Indonesian). The Burmese editions were repeatedly denounced by the Burmese military dictators, and the Indonesian edition carried a Foreword by Abdurrahman Wahid, now President of Indonesia. The Spanish translation circulates in Cuba.

Dr. Sharp has in recent years made major efforts to prepare simplified presentations on the nature of nonviolent struggle and its applications against dictatorships. He has conducted workshops and consulted on strategic nonviolent struggle in several crisis situations.

He maintains that the major unsolved political problems of our time—dictatorship, genocide, war, social oppression, and popular powerlessness—require us to rethink politics in order to develop fresh strategies and programs for their resolution. He is convinced that pragmatic, strategically planned, nonviolent struggle can be made highly effective for application in conflicts to lift oppression and as a substitute for violence.

*For more information on the works of Gene Sharp, contact:*

THE ALBERT EINSTEIN INSTITUTION
427 Newbury Street
Boston, MA 02115-1801
Tel: (617) 247-4882   Fax: (617) 247-4035
Web: www.aeinstein.org   E-mail: einstein@igc.org

*See the last page for information on ordering other Sharp titles from Porter Sargent Publishers, Inc.*

# Preface

There is no pretense that this study is exhaustive. The historical material on nonviolent action which is used here only scratches the surface of past experience, for example. This volume is, however, the most comprehensive attempt thus far to examine the nature of nonviolent struggle as a social and political technique, including its view of power, its specific methods of action, its dynamics in conflict and the conditions for success or failure in its use. The historical material is used primarily in assisting the inductive construction of the analyses, theories and hypotheses. It is hoped that this book will stimulate many other studies and explorations of the nature of this technique and of its potentialities as a substitute for political violence.

This study was begun out of a view that alternatives to violence in meeting tyranny, aggression, injustice and oppression are needed. At the same time it appeared evident that both moral injunctions against violence and exhortations in favor of love and nonviolence have made little or no contribution to ending war and major political violence. It seemed to me that only the adoption of a substitute type of sanction and struggle as a functional alternative to violence in acute conflicts—where important issues are, or are believed to be, at stake—could possibly lead to a major reduction of political violence in a manner compatible with freedom, justice and human dignity.

But mere advocacy of nonviolent alternatives will not necessarily produce any change either—unless they are accurately perceived as being at least as effective as the violent alternatives. That, too, is not a matter for sermonizing or declarations. Therefore, a very careful examination of the nature, capacities and requirements of nonviolent struggle was necessary, which needed to be as objective as possible. This study is my primary contribution to that task. This work should not be regarded as final, but as a tool for increasing our understanding and knowledge; its propositions, classifications, analyses and hypotheses should be subjected to further examination, research and critical analysis.

Since this book is focused almost exclusively on the nature of the nonviolent technique of action, several closely related areas are not treated here. For example, relationships between this technique and ethical problems, and between the technique and belief systems exhorting to nonviolent behavior, are for the most part not discussed here. This study may be, however, the basis for a fresh look at those problems.[1] The political implications and potentialities of nonviolent action, including for social change and for national defense,[2] have also been left for separate exploration; it is hoped that this study will assist those investigations.[3]

This book is the culmination of studies which began in 1950 while I was a student at Ohio State University. A lengthy draft of a book manuscript with the present title was completed at St. Catherine's College, Oxford in 1963, partially based on work done earlier in Norway, first at the Institute of Philosophy and the History of Ideas of the University of Oslo, and, then, for two-and-a-half years, at the Institute for Social Research. After much further research, a full revision and expansion of major parts of the 1963 draft was completed in 1968 at the Center for International Affairs of Harvard University. This became also my doctoral thesis at the University of Oxford, for which I was awarded the degree of D. Phil. in November 1968. This book is a thorough revision and rewriting of that 1968 thesis, with expansion of certain chapters and a restructuring of the whole book and of individual chapters. That rewriting took nearly three years further due to teaching responsibilities.

This study has been possible because of the encouragement and assistance of others. My parents, Eva M. and Paul W. Sharp, merit first place in thanks for their understanding and kindnesses in many ways over the years.

Most of the research and drafting has been done at four institutions: the Institute for Social Research in Oslo, Norway; the Institute of Philosophy and the History of Ideas of the University of Oslo; St. Catherine's College of the University of Oxford; and the Center for International Affairs of Harvard University; each of these, the members of their staffs and faculties, and their libraries deserve special appreciation. Mr. Erik Rinde, former Director of the Institute for Social Research, merits individual mention.

Very particular gratitude is also due to five men whose encouragement, help, advice, and infinite patience at various stages enabled me to continue study of this field: Professor Kurt H. Wolff of Brandeis University; Professor Arne Naess of the University of Oslo; Mr. Alan Bullock, Master of St. Catherine's College and Vice-Chancellor of the University of Oxford; Professor John Plamenatz of All Souls College, Oxford; and Professor Thomas C. Schelling of the Center for International Affairs of Harvard University, and now Chairman of the Public Policy Program of the John F. Kennedy School of Government of Harvard University. Without their help I could not have carried on.

Thanks must also go to the various sources of financial assistance which provided funds and loans over the years to enable me to continue.

I should also like to thank for their various kindnesses Sir Isaiah Berlin, President, Wolfson College, Oxford; Mr. Wilfrid Knapp and Mr. B. E. F. Fender of St. Catherine's College, Oxford; the members of the Board of the Faculty of Social Studies of the University of Oxford; Mr. Christopher Seton-Watson of Oriel College, Oxford; Professor J. C. Rees of University College, Swansea (then visiting All Souls College, Oxford); Dr. Robert L. Jervis of the Center for International Affairs of Harvard University; and Dean Richard Fontera of Southeastern Massachusetts University. Most of the individual academic acknowledgements are made in footnotes, but George Lakey and John L. Sorenson—both of whom have researched in this field—should be mentioned here for their suggestions of specific methods or examples which have been incorporated in the text and are not specifically credited. Individual members of the staff of the Center for International Affairs who merit special mention for help in typing, proofreading, reproduction and suggestions are Moira Clarke, Margaret Rothwell, James Havlin, Katherine Brest and especially Jeanette Asdourian. Dennis Brady searched libraries to help provide references to pagination in both British and American editions wherever possible.

The index has been prepared by John Hearn, William Singleton, Walter Conser, Ronald McCarthy, Ken Feldman and myself. Ronald McCarthy also ably assisted in other ways in getting the final manuscript to press, including steps in the obtaining of permissions for quotations. Walter Conser and Jessie

Jones helped considerably in proofreading and other tasks. From Porter Sargent Publisher, I wish to thank for their kindnesses and assistance in various ways Debbie Rose, Pat Roberts, Tom Murray, Jan Boddie, Jennie Fonzo, and F. Porter Sargent himself. Robert Reitherman, formerly a student at Harvard University, has drawn the charts and helped in diverse ways, not the least of which was encouragement. This also came generously from April Carter, Theodor Ebert, Adam Roberts and Sandi Tatman who volunteered special advice and help. Various of my students, from the University of Massachusetts at Boston, Tufts University, Brandeis University, Harvard University and Southeastern Massachusetts University, have offered helpful comments and suggestions.

During four of my years as Research Associate and Research Fellow at the Center for International Affairs of Harvard University, while the 1968 draft was being completed, I received funds from grants for projects of Professor Thomas C. Schelling made to Harvard University from the Ford Foundation and from the Advanced Research Projects Agency of the U.S. Department of Defense, Contract No. F44620-67-C-0011. Some persons may find either the availability or the acceptance of such funds surprising; I have been arguing for years that governments and defense departments—as well as other groups—should finance and conduct research into alternatives to violence in politics and especially as a possible basis for a defense policy by prepared nonviolent resistance as a substitute for war. As acceptance of such Defense Department funds involved no restrictions whatever on the research, writing, or dissemination of the results, I willingly accepted them. I welcome further research by governments and defense departments of all countries into alternatives to violence and war. After the completion of that draft, the Center for International Affairs provided an office and typing and editorial assistance for the rewriting of this volume.

The final rewriting of this book has only been possible because of the perceptive intellect, skillful pen, and friendly candor of Dr. Marina S. Finkelstein, Editor of Publications at the Center from 1968 until her death in 1972.

It is my hope that this book will serve as a contribution to the beginning of new research, investigation and development of effective nonviolent alternatives to domestic violence and international war.

Gene Sharp
Harvard University
Center for International Affairs
Cambridge, Massachusetts
June 1972.

# NOTES

1. See Gene Sharp, "Ethics and Responsibility in Politics: A critique of the present adequacy of Max Weber's classification of ethical systems," in **Inquiry** (Oslo), vol. VII, no. 3 (Autumn 1964), pp. 304-317; Gene Sharp, "Dilemmas of Morality in Politics," in **Reconciliation Quarterly** (London), First Quarter 1965, no. 128, pp. 528-535; Reinhold Niebuhr. **Moral Man and Immoral Society** (New York: Charles Scribner's Sons, 1960 [orig. 1932] and London: S.C.M. Press, 1963) pp. 167, 238, 250-251, and 254; Gene Sharp, "Gandhi's Defence Policy," in T. K. Mahadevan, Adam Roberts and Gene Sharp, eds., **Civilian Defence: An Introduction** (Bombay: Bharatiya Vidya Bhavan and New Delhi: Gandhi Peace Foundation, 1967), pp. 15-52; and Gene Sharp, "Non-violence: Moral Principle or Political Technique?" in **Indian Political Science Review** (Delhi), vol. IV, no. 1 (Oct. 1969-Mar. 1970), pp. 17-36. On belief systems which reject violence, see Gene Sharp, "Types of Principled Nonviolence" in A. Paul Hare and Herbert H. Blumberg, eds., **Nonviolent Direct Action: American Cases: Social-Psychological Analyses** (Washington, D.C. and Cleveland: Corpus Books, 1968), pp. 273-313.
2. For introductory studies of civilian defense, see Gene Sharp **"The Political Equivalent of War"–Civilian Defense,** 67 pp., **International Conciliation,** no. 555 (Nov. 1965, whole issue), New York: Carnegie Endowment for International Peace; Gene Sharp, **Exploring Nonviolent Alternatives** (Boston: Porter Sargent, 1970), pp. 47-72; and Adam Roberts, ed., **Civilian Resistance as a National Defense** (Harrisburg, Pa.: Stackpole Books, 1968; paperback: Harmondsworth, Middlesex, England and Baltimore, Md.: Penquin Books, 1969). Original British edition titled **The Strategy of Civilian Defense** (London: Faber & Faber, 1967).
3. For research areas on nonviolent action and its application, see Sharp, **Exploring Nonviolent Alternatives,** pp. 73-113. For a classified guide to the existing literature, see *ibid.,* pp. 133-159.

# CONTENTS

PREFACE  *by Dr. Gene Sharp*                                                      v

INTRODUCTION  *by Professor Thomas C. Schelling*                                  xix


## PART ONE: POWER AND STRUGGLE

INTRODUCTION                                                                       3


### Chapter One
### THE NATURE AND CONTROL OF POLITICAL POWER

INTRODUCTION                                      7

WHAT IS THE BASIC NATURE OF
POLITICAL POWER?                                  8

SOCIAL ROOTS OF POLITICAL
POWER                                            10
A.  *Sources of power*                           11
   1.  Authority                  11
   2.  Human resources            11
   3.  Skills and knowledge       11
   4.  Intangible factors         11
   5.  Material resources         11
   6.  Sanctions                  12
B.  *These sources depend on*
   *obedience*                     12

WHY DO MEN OBEY?                                 16
A.  *The reasons are various*
   *and multiple*                  19
   1.  Habit                       19
   2.  Fear of sanctions          19
   3.  Moral obligation           20
   4.  Self-interest              22
   5.  Psychological identification
      with the ruler  23
   6.  Zones of indifference      23
   7.  Absence of self-confidence
      among subjects  23
B.  *Obtaining the ruler's functionaries*
   *and agents*                     24

C.  *Obedience is not inevitable*                25

THE ROLE OF CONSENT                              25
A.  *Obedience is essentially voluntary*         26
B.  *Consent can be withdrawn*                   30

TOWARD A THEORY OF
NONVIOLENT CONTROL OF
POLITICAL POWER                                  32
A.  *Traditional controls*                       32
   1.  Self-restraint             33
   2.  Institutional arrangements  33
   3.  Applying superior means
      of violence   34
B.  *Theorists on withdrawal*
   *of support*                     34
C.  *Clues to the political impact of*
   *noncooperation*                 36
   1.  Bureaucratic obstruction    36
      The United States  36
*Chart One:* Power                               37
      The Soviet Union  39
      Germany         40
   2.  Popular noncooperation      41
      India           41
      The Soviet Union  42
D.  *Toward a technique of control of*
   *political power*                43

NOTES TO CHAPTER ONE                             48

# Chapter Two

## NONVIOLENT ACTION: AN ACTIVE TECHNIQUE OF STRUGGLE

INTRODUCTION 63
CHARACTERISTICS OF
NONVIOLENT ACTION 64
A. *A special type of action* 64
*Chart Two:* Action in Conflicts 66
B. *Motives, methods, and leverages* 67
C. *Correcting misconceptions* 70
D. *A neglected type of struggle* 71
ILLUSTRATIONS FROM THE PAST 75
A. *Some early historical examples* 75
B. *The pre-Gandhian expansion*
*of nonviolent struggle* 76
C. *Early twentieth-century cases* 78
  1. Russian Empire–1905-06 78
  2. Berlin–1920 79
  3. The *Ruhrkampf* – 1923 81
D. *Gandhi's contribution* 82
  1. Vykom–1924-25 83

  2. Gandhi's theory of power 83
  3. India–1930-31 86
E. *Struggles against Nazis* 87
  1. Norway–1942 88
  2. Berlin–1943 89
F. *Latin American civilian*
  *insurrections* 90
  1. Guatemala–1944 90
G. *Rising against Communist regimes* 93
  1. Vorkuta–1953 93
H. *American civil rights struggles* 95
  1. Montgomery, Alabama–
    1955-56 95
CONTINUING DEVELOPMENT 97
A. *Czechoslovakia–1968* 98
SEEKING INSIGHT 101

NOTES TO CHAPTER TWO 102

## PART TWO: THE METHODS OF NONVIOLENT ACTION
## POLITICAL JIU-JITSU AT WORK

INTRODUCTION 109
NOTES 115

# Chapter Three

## THE METHODS OF NONVIOLENT PROTEST AND PERSUASION

INTRODUCTION 117
FORMAL STATEMENTS 119
  1. Public speeches 119
  2. Letters of opposition or
    support 120
  3. Declarations by organizations
    and institutions 121
  4. Signed public statements 122
  5. Declarations of indictment
    and intention 123
  6. Group or mass petitions 123
COMMUNICATIONS WITH A
WIDER AUDIENCE 125
  7. Slogans, caricatures and
    symbols 125
  8. Banners, posters and
    displayed communications 126
  9. Leaflets, pamphlets and
    books 127
  10. Newspapers and journals 128

  11. Records, radio and television 129
  12. Skywriting and earthwriting 130
GROUP REPRESENTATIONS 130
  13. Deputations 130
  14. Mock awards 131
  15. Group lobbying 132
  16. Picketing 132
  17. Mock elections 134
SYMBOLIC PUBLIC ACTS 135
  18. Displays of flags and
    symbolic colors 135
  19. Wearing of symbols 136
  20. Prayer and worship 137
  21. Delivering symbolic objects 139
  22. Protest disrobings 140
  23. Destruction of own property 140
  24. Symbolic lights 142
  25. Displays of portraits 143
  26. Paint as protest 143
  27. New signs and names 143

| | | |
|---|---|---|
| 28. | Symbolic sounds | 144 |
| 29. | Symbolic reclamations | 145 |
| 30. | Rude gestures | 145 |
| **PRESSURES ON INDIVIDUALS** | | 145 |
| 31. | "Haunting" officials | 145 |
| 32. | Taunting officials | 146 |
| 33. | Fraternization | 146 |
| 34. | Vigils | 147 |
| **DRAMA AND MUSIC** | | 148 |
| 35. | Humorous skits and pranks | 148 |
| 36. | Performances of plays and music | 149 |
| 37. | Singing | 149 |
| **PROCESSIONS** | | 152 |
| 38. | Marches | 152 |
| 39. | Parades | 154 |
| 40. | Religious processions | 155 |
| 41. | Pilgrimages | 156 |
| 42. | Motorcades | 156 |

| | | |
|---|---|---|
| **HONORING THE DEAD** | | 157 |
| 43. | Political mourning | 157 |
| 44. | Mock funerals | 158 |
| 45. | Demonstrative funerals | 159 |
| 46. | Homage at burial places | 162 |
| **PUBLIC ASSEMBLIES** | | 163 |
| 47. | Assemblies of protest or support | 163 |
| 48. | Protest meetings | 165 |
| 49. | Camouflaged meetings of protest | 167 |
| 50. | Teach-ins | 169 |
| **WITHDRAWAL AND RENUNCIATION** | | 169 |
| 51. | Walk-outs | 169 |
| 52. | Silence | 170 |
| 53. | Renouncing honors | 171 |
| 54. | Turning one's back | 172 |
| **NOTES TO CHAPTER THREE** | | 173 |

Chapter Four

## THE METHODS OF SOCIAL NONCOOPERATION

| | | |
|---|---|---|
| **INTRODUCTION** | | 183 |
| **OSTRACISM OF PERSONS** | | 184 |
| 55. | Social boycott | 184 |
| 56. | Selective social boycott | 190 |
| 57. | Lysistratic nonaction | 191 |
| 58. | Excommunication | 191 |
| 59. | Interdict | 192 |
| **NONCOOPERATION WITH SOCIAL EVENTS, CUSTOMS AND INSTITUTIONS** | | 193 |
| 60. | Suspension of social and sports activities | 193 |
| 61. | Boycott of social affairs | 196 |

| | | |
|---|---|---|
| 62. | Student strike | 196 |
| 63. | Social disobedience | 198 |
| 64. | Withdrawal from social institutions | 199 |
| **WITHDRAWAL FROM THE SOCIAL SYSTEM** | | 199 |
| 65. | Stay-at-home | 199 |
| 66. | Total personal noncooperation | 200 |
| 67. | "Flight" of workers | 201 |
| 68. | Sanctuary | 204 |
| 69. | Collective disappearance | 210 |
| 70. | Protest emigration (*hijrat*) | 211 |
| **NOTES TO CHAPTER FOUR** | | 214 |

Chapter Five

## THE METHODS OF ECONOMIC NONCOOPERATION: (1) ECONOMIC BOYCOTTS

| | | |
|---|---|---|
| **INTRODUCTION** | | 219 |
| **ACTION BY CONSUMERS** | | 221 |
| 71. | Consumers' boycott | 221 |
| 72. | Nonconsumption of boycotted goods | 224 |
| 73. | Policy of austerity | 225 |
| 74. | Rent withholding | 226 |
| 75. | Refusal to rent | 228 |
| 76. | National consumers' boycott | 228 |
| 77. | International consumers' boycott | 230 |

| | | |
|---|---|---|
| **ACTION BY WORKERS AND PRODUCERS** | | 230 |
| 78. | Workmen's boycott | 230 |
| 79. | Producers' boycott | 231 |
| **ACTION BY MIDDLEMEN** | | 232 |
| 80. | Suppliers' and handlers' boycott | 232 |
| **ACTION BY OWNERS AND MANAGEMENT** | | 234 |
| 81. | Traders' boycott | 234 |
| 82. | Refusal to let or sell property | 235 |

| | | |
|---|---|---|
| 83. | Lockout | 235 |
| 84. | Refusal of industrial assistance | 236 |
| 85. | Merchants' "general strike" | 236 |

**ACTION BY HOLDERS OF FINANCIAL RESOURCES**    236

| | | |
|---|---|---|
| 86. | Withdrawal of bank deposits | 236 |
| 87. | Refusal to pay fees, dues, and assessments | 237 |
| 88. | Refusal to pay debts or interest | 237 |
| 89. | Severance of funds and credit | 239 |
| 90. | Revenue refusal | 240 |
| 91. | Refusal of a government's money | 244 |

**ACTION BY GOVERNMENTS**    244

| | | |
|---|---|---|
| 92. | Domestic embargo | 244 |
| 93. | Blacklisting of traders | 244 |
| 94. | International sellers' embargo | 245 |
| 95. | International buyers' embargo | 246 |
| 96. | International trade embargo | 246 |

**NOTES TO CHAPTER FIVE**    249

Chapter Six

# THE METHODS OF ECONOMIC NONCOOPERATION: (2) THE STRIKE

**INTRODUCTION**    257

**SYMBOLIC STRIKES**    259

| | | |
|---|---|---|
| 97. | Protest strike | 259 |
| 98. | Quickie walkout (lightning strike) | 261 |

**AGRICULTURAL STRIKES**    261

| | | |
|---|---|---|
| 99. | Peasant strike | 261 |
| 100. | Farm workers' strike | 262 |

**STRIKES BY SPECIAL GROUPS**    264

| | | |
|---|---|---|
| 101. | Refusal of impressed labor | 264 |
| 102. | Prisoners' strike | 265 |
| 103. | Craft strike | 265 |
| 104. | Professional strike | 265 |

**ORDINARY INDUSTRIAL STRIKES**    267

| | | |
|---|---|---|
| 105. | Establishment strike | 267 |
| 106. | Industry strike | 267 |
| 107. | Sympathetic strike | 267 |

**RESTRICTED STRIKES**    268

| | | |
|---|---|---|
| 108. | Detailed strike | 268 |
| 109. | Bumper strike | 269 |
| 110. | Slowdown strike | 269 |
| 111. | Working-to-rule strike | 271 |
| 112. | Reporting "sick" (sick-in) | 271 |
| 113. | Strike by resignation | 273 |
| 114. | Limited strike | 273 |
| 115. | Selective strike | 274 |

**MULTI-INDUSTRY STRIKES**    275

| | | |
|---|---|---|
| 116. | Generalized strike | 275 |
| 117. | General strike | 275 |

**COMBINATION OF STRIKES AND ECONOMIC CLOSURES**    277

| | | |
|---|---|---|
| 118. | Hartal | 277 |
| 119. | Economic shutdown | 278 |

**NOTES TO CHAPTER SIX**    280

Chapter Seven

# THE METHODS OF POLITICAL NONCOOPERATION

**INTRODUCTION**    285

**REJECTION OF AUTHORITY**    286

| | | |
|---|---|---|
| 120. | Withholding or withdrawal of allegiance | 286 |
| 121. | Refusal of public support | 288 |
| 122. | Literature and speeches advocating resistance | 289 |

**CITIZENS' NONCOOPERATION WITH GOVERNMENT**    289

| | | |
|---|---|---|
| 123. | Boycott of legislative bodies | 289 |
| 124. | Boycott of elections | 291 |
| 125. | Boycott of government employment and positions | 292 |
| 126. | Boycott of government departments, agencies and other bodies | 295 |
| 127. | Withdrawal from government educational institutions | 297 |
| 128. | Boycott of government-supported organizations | 298 |
| 129. | Refusal of assistance to enforcement agents | 298 |
| 130. | Removal of own signs and placemarks | 300 |
| 131. | Refusal to accept appointed officials | 301 |
| 132. | Refusal to dissolve existing institutions | 302 |

CITIZENS' ALTERNATIVES TO
OBEDIENCE                                303
133. Reluctant and slow compliance      303
134. Nonobedience in absence of
     direct supervision                  304
135. Popular nonobedience               304
136. Disguised disobedience             306
137. Refusal of an assemblage
     or meeting to disperse             308
138. Sitdown                            310
139. Noncooperation with
     conscription and deportation        311
140. Hiding, escape and false
     identities                          313
141. Civil disobedience of
     "illegitimate" laws                315
ACTION BY GOVERNMENT
PERSONNEL                                320
142. Selective refusal of assistance
     by government aides                320
143. Blocking of lines of command
     and information                     321
144. Stalling and obstruction           323
145. General administrative
     noncooperation                      328
146. Judicial noncooperation            328
147. Deliberate inefficiency and
     selective noncooperation by

enforcement agents                       330
148. Mutiny                             332
DOMESTIC GOVERNMENTAL
ACTION                                   335
149. Quasi-legal evasions and
     delays                              335
150. Noncooperation by
     constituent governmental
     units                               337
INTERNATIONAL
GOVERNMENTAL ACTION                      340
151. Changes in diplomatic and
     other representation               340
152. Delay and cancellation of
     diplomatic events                  341
153. Withholding of diplomatic
     recognition                         342
154. Severance of diplomatic
     relations                           344
155. Withdrawal from international
     organizations                       345
156. Refusal of membership in
     international bodies                346
157. Expulsion from international
     organizations                       346

NOTES TO CHAPTER SEVEN          347

## Chapter Eight

## THE METHODS OF NONVIOLENT INTERVENTION

INTRODUCTION                             357
PSYCHOLOGICAL
INTERVENTION                             359
158. Self-exposure to the elements      359
159. The fast                           360
     (a)  Fast of moral pressure        360
     (b)  Hunger strike                 363
     (c)  Satyagrahic fast              367
160. Reverse trial                      368
161. Nonviolent harassment             369
PHYSICAL INTERVENTION                    371
162. Sit-in                             371
163. Stand-in                           374
164. Ride-in                            375
165. Wade-in                            378
166. Mill-in                            378
167. Pray-in                            379
168. Nonviolent raids                   380
169. Nonviolent air raids               381
170. Nonviolent invasion               382
171. Nonviolent interjection           382
172. Nonviolent obstruction            387

173. Nonviolent occupation             388
SOCIAL INTERVENTION                      390
174. Establishing new social
     patterns                            390
175. Overloading of facilities         393
176. Stall-in                           394
177. Speak-in                           395
178. Guerrilla theater                  397
179. Alternative social institutions   398
180. Alternative communication
     system                              400
ECONOMIC INTERVENTION                    401
181. Reverse strike                     402
182. Stay-in strike                     403
183. Nonviolent land seizure           405
184. Defiance of blockades             408
185. Politically motivated
     counterfeiting                      409
186. Preclusive purchasing             410
187. Seizure of assets                 410
188. Dumping                            411
189. Selective patronage               412

190. Alternative markets 413
191. Alternative transportation systems 414
192. Alternative economic institutions 415
POLITICAL INTERVENTION 416
193. Overloading of administrative systems 416
194. Disclosing identities of secret agents 418

195. Seeking imprisonment 418
196. Civil disobedience of "neutral" laws 420
197. Work-on without collaboration 421
198. Dual sovereignty and parallel government 423
CONCLUSION 433

NOTES TO CHAPTER EIGHT 435

## PART THREE: THE DYNAMICS OF NONVIOLENT ACTION

INTRODUCTION 449
NOTES 450

Chapter Nine

# LAYING THE GROUNDWORK FOR NONVIOLENT ACTION

INTRODUCTION 451
CONFRONTING THE OPPONENT'S POWER 451
RISKS AND VARIATIONS IN NONVIOLENT ACTION 454
CASTING OFF FEAR 456
SOCIAL SOURCES OF POWER CHANGES 458
LEADERSHIP IN NONVIOLENT STRUGGLE 462
PREPARING FOR NONVIOLENT STRUGGLE 467
A. Investigation 468
B. Negotiations 469
C. Sharpening the focus for attack 471
D. Generating "cause-consciousness" 473
E. Quantity and quality in nonviolent action 475
F. Organizing the movement 479
OPENNESS AND SECRECY IN

NONVIOLENT STRUGGLE 481
BASIC ELEMENTS IN NONVIOLENT STRATEGY 492
A. The importance of strategy and tactics 493
B. Some key elements in nonviolent strategy and tactics 495
    1. The indirect approach to the opponent's power 495
    2. Psychological elements 496
    3. Geographical and physical elements 496
    4. Timing 497
    5. Numbers and strength 498
    6. The issue and concentration of strength 499
    7. The initiative 500
C. The choice of weapons 501
D. Selecting the strategy and tactics 504
THE ULTIMATUM 510

NOTES TO CHAPTER NINE 514

Chapter Ten

# CHALLENGE BRINGS REPRESSION

INTRODUCTION 521
A HALT TO SUBMISSION 522
INITIAL POLARIZATION FOLLOWED BY SHIFTING POWER 524
THE OPPONENT'S INITIAL PROBLEM 528

REPRESSION 537
A. Control of communication and information 538
B. Psychological pressures 538
C. Confiscation 538
D. Economic sanctions 538
E. Bans and prohibitions 538
F. Arrests and imprisonments 539

| | | | | |
|---|---|---|---|---|
| G. | *Exceptional restrictions* | 539 | FACING BRUTALITIES | 555 |
| H. | *Direct physical violence* | 539 | A. *Official and unofficial brutalities* | 556 |
| | PERSISTENCE | 547 | B. *Remaining firm* | 562 |
| | THE NECESSITY OF SUFFERING | 551 | NOTES TO CHAPTER TEN | 566 |

## Chapter Eleven

## SOLIDARITY AND DISCIPLINE TO FIGHT REPRESSION

| | | | |
|---|---|---|---|
| INTRODUCTION | 573 | SABOTAGE AND NONVIOLENT | |
| THE NEED FOR SOLIDARITY | 573 | ACTION | 608 |
| A. *Maintaining rapport* | 575 | OTHER WAYS TO SLIP INTO | |
| B. *Generating incentives* | 577 | VIOLENCE | 611 |
| C. *Reducing grounds for* | | THE NECESSITY OF DISCIPLINE | 615 |
| *capitulation* | 578 | PROMOTING NONVIOLENT | |
| D. *Restraints or sanctions* | 580 | DISCIPLINE | 620 |
| INHIBITING REPRESSION | 583 | REFUSAL TO HATE | 633 |
| THE OPPONENT PREFERS | | THE INEFFICACY OF | |
| VIOLENCE | 586 | REPRESSION | 636 |
| THE NEED FOR NONVIOLENT | | A. *Arresting leaders is inadequate* | 636 |
| BEHAVIOR | 594 | B. *Repression measures may be-* | |
| HOW VIOLENCE WEAKENS THE | | *come new points of resistance* | 640 |
| MOVEMENT | 597 | NOTES TO CHAPTER ELEVEN | 643 |

## Chapter Twelve

## POLITICAL JIU-JITSU

| | | | |
|---|---|---|---|
| INTRODUCTION | 657 | F. *Provocation and appeals* | 677 |
| WINNING OVER UNCOMMITTED | | INCREASING SUPPORT AND | |
| THIRD PARTIES | 658 | PARTICIPATION FROM THE | |
| A. *International indignation* | 659 | GRIEVANCE GROUP | 678 |
| B. *Factors determining the impact* | | A. *The victory in Palace Square* | 678 |
| *of third-party opinion* | 662 | B. *Strength needed to withstand* | |
| C. *The future of third-party support* | 664 | *repression* | 680 |
| AROUSING DISSENT AND | | C. *Repression may legitimize* | |
| OPPOSITION IN THE OPPONENT'S | | *resistance* | 681 |
| OWN CAMP | 665 | D. *The numbers of resisters may* | |
| A. *Questioning both repression and* | | *grow* | 682 |
| *the cause* | 665 | LESS SEVERE REPRESSION AND | |
| B. *Repression produces defections:* | | COUNTER-NONVIOLENCE? | 690 |
| *three cases* | 667 | ALTERING POWER | |
| C. *Four more cases of defections* | 669 | RELATIONSHIPS | 695 |
| D. *The troops mutiny* | 671 | | |
| E. *Splits in the opponent regime* | 675 | NOTES TO CHAPTER TWELVE | 698 |

## Chapter Thirteen

## THREE WAYS SUCCESS MAY BE ACHIEVED

| | | | |
|---|---|---|---|
| INTRODUCTION | 705 | C. *The barrier of social distance* | 711 |
| CONVERSION | 707 | D. *Conversion through self-suffering* | 717 |
| A. *Seeking conversion* | 707 | E. *Some factors influencing* | |
| B. *The rationale of self-suffering* | 709 | *conversion* | 726 |

**CONTENTS** *xvii*

| | | |
|---|---|---|
| 1. External factors | 726 | |
| 2. Internal factors | 727 | |
| F. *Conversion may not be achieved* | 731 | |
| ACCOMMODATION | 733 | |
| A. *Violent repression seen as inappropriate* | 734 | |
| B. *Getting rid of a nuisance* | 735 | |
| C. *Adjusting to opposition in his own group* | 736 | |
| D. *Minimizing economic losses* | 737 | |
| E. *Bowing gracefully to the inevitable* | 738 | |
| NONVIOLENT COERCION | 741 | |
| A. *The concept of nonviolent coercion* | 742 | |
| B. *Withdrawing the sources of* | | |

| | |
|---|---|
| *political power* | 744 |
| 1. Authority | 745 |
| 2. Human resources | 746 |
| 3. Skills and knowledge | 747 |
| 4. Intangible factors | 749 |
| 5. Material resources | 750 |
| 6. Sanctions | 752 |
| C. *Some factors influencing nonviolent coercion* | 754 |
| A SUCCESSFUL CONCLUSION? | 755 |
| A. *The risk and nature of defeat* | 756 |
| B. *A draw or an interim settlement?* | 758 |
| C. *Success* | 764 |
| D. *Toward a genuine solution* | 767 |
| NOTES TO CHAPTER THIRTEEN | 769 |

Chapter Fourteen

## THE REDISTRIBUTION OF POWER

| | | |
|---|---|---|
| INTRODUCTION | 777 | |
| EFFECTS ON THE NONVIOLENT GROUP | 777 | |
| A. *Ending submissiveness* | 778 | |
| B. *Learning a technique which reveals one's power* | 779 | |
| C. *Increasing fearlessness* | 782 | |
| D. *Increased self-esteem* | 784 | |
| E. *Bringing satisfaction, enthusiasm and hope* | 787 | |
| F. *Effects on aggression, masculinity, crime and violence* | 789 | |
| G. *Increased group unity* | 793 | |

| | |
|---|---|
| H. *Increased internal cooperation* | 795 |
| I. *Contagion* | 798 |
| J. *Conclusion* | 799 |
| DIFFUSED POWER AND THE NONVIOLENT TECHNIQUE | 799 |
| A. *Violence and centralization of power* | 800 |
| B. *Nonviolent action and decentralization of power* | 802 |
| CONCLUSION | 806 |
| NOTES TO CHAPTER FOURTEEN | 811 |

| | | | |
|---|---|---|---|
| APPENDIX | 815 | INDEX | 841 |
| BIBLIOGRAPHY | 819 | ACKNOWLEDGMENTS | 895 |

# Introduction

## by Professor Thomas C. Schelling, Harvard University

The original idea was to subject the entire theory of nonviolent political action, together with a full history of its practice in all parts of the world since the time of Christ, to the same cool, detailed scrutiny that military strategy and tactics are supposed to invite. Now that we have Gene Sharp's book, what we lack is an equally comprehensive, careful study of the politics of violent action.

Violence gets plenty of attention. But purposive violence, violence for political effect, is rarely examined in print with anything like the care and comprehensiveness, the attention to detail and the wealth of historical examples, that Gene Sharp brings to nonviolent action.

It is too bad that we haven't that other book, the one on violent action. It would be good to compare the two in detail. This book's analysis of nonviolent action might be even more impressive if it had a competitor.

Nonviolence can hardly compete with violence in total effect—it rarely produces disasters of the magnitude that violence has made familiar—but what we would want to compare is not some gross potency but the achievement of political purpose and the costs of the achievement. And we would need detailed comparisons in a multitude of contexts, to learn the strengths and weaknesses of both kinds of action in differing circumstances.

The difference is not like the difference between prayer and dynamite. Political violence, like political nonviolence, usually has as its purpose making somebody do something or not do something or stop doing something. The aim is to influence behavior. Violent action tries to do it mainly by intimidating people—large numbers or a few, followers or leaders, common citizens or officials. (The people to be intimidated need not be the direct victims of the violence.) The violence does not directly make people behave or perform or participate; it can only make it hurt if they don't. Indeed, the most skillful use of violence may produce, precisely because it is skillful, comparatively little violence.

The violent actions and the nonviolent are different methods of trying to make it unrewarding for people to do certain things, and safe or rewarding to do other things. Both can be misused, mishandled, or misapplied. Both can be used for evil or misguided purposes. "Nonviolent action" furthermore, as developed in this book, is not merely all the kinds of political activity in which violence is absent or unintended; so "violent action" and "nonviolent action" do not exhaust the possibilities. A comparison of the two would not be just a way of picking a favorite, but rather a way of highlighting similarities and differences in different contexts and illuminating political processes themselves.

This book does shed some light on the theory of violent action. The more coercive nonviolent techniques, in particular, have something in common with the techniques based on violence. (They can even entail a latent threat of violence, although often it is the people "nonviolently" posing the threat who would be the victims if violence broke out.)

Discipline, command and control; intelligence about the adversary; careful choice of weapons, targets, terrain and time of day; and, especially, avoiding impetuous recourse to provoked or purposeless violence, are critical to success in violent as in nonviolent action. Most of what are usually called the "principles of war" are chapter headings rather than rules to follow—things like economy, concentration, purpose, initiative, and surprise—and, as topical headings, are about as appropriate to the study of nonviolent action as to the violent.

One of the main differences is that violent action often requires hot blood, while the nonviolent depends more on cool heads. That is why the violent is so much easier to engage in, but perhaps harder to engage in with a clear and sustained consciousness of purpose. The violent tends to make demands on morale that are incompatible with dispassionate calculation or continual assessment of goals. The victims of violence get to be seen as enemies or criminals. The scoring system is corrupted; and accomplishment comes to be measured negatively, by how much an enemy has been frustrated and hurt, not by how effectively someone has been influenced into accommodating, participating, or whatever it was that the violence was supposed to make him do.

There is probably a corresponding effect in nonviolence, a tendency to count one's own risk and suffering as accomplishment. But in terms of effectiveness, as political action, neither the hurting nor the being hurt should be mistaken as the ultimate goal or the accomplishment of political purpose.

What Gene Sharp's book does at every step is to relate the methods of nonviolent action, and the organizational requirements, the logistics and the leadership and the discipline, the recruitment of members and the choice of targets, to political purpose. Nonviolence as a source of sheer personal gratification gets little attention, just as inflicting pain for its own sake, as sheer retribution, should get little attention in that other book on the politics of violent action.

The book does not attempt to convert you to a new faith. It is not about a compassionate political philosophy that, if only enough of us believed it, would make the walls come tumbling down. It offers insight, by theory and example, into a complex field of strategy. There is a coherence to the theory and an integrity to the book as a whole; but no one has to accept all the principles developed or to assume the author's point of view in order to get a new appreciation of politics and its methods. The book offers insight into the past and it illuminates a multitude of contemporary events that, whether or not they affect us, we are witnesses to. And many of them do affect us. And some of them we are engaged in.

And if the book should fall into the wrong hands, and begin to inform and enlighten our adversaries, we can be doubly thankful for the work Gene Sharp has done. Whatever the contest, there is a good chance that one is better off confronting a skillful and effective recourse to nonviolent action than a savagely ineffectual resort to violence.

# PART ONE:
# Power and Struggle

# INTRODUCTION
## TO PART ONE

Some conflicts do not yield to compromise and can be resolved only through struggle. Conflicts which, in one way or another, involve the fundamental principles of a society, of independence, of self-respect, or of people's capacity to determine their own future are such conflicts. For their resolution, regular institutional procedures are rarely available; it is even doubtful that they could be completely adequate. Instead, in the belief that the choice in these types of conflicts is between abject passive surrender and violence, and also that victory requires violence, people turn to the threat and use of violence. The specific means used will vary: they may include conventional military action, guerrilla warfare, regicide, rioting, police action, private armed offense and defense, civil war, terrorism, conventional aerial bombings and nuclear attacks, as well as other forms. Whether threatened, used with restraint, or applied without controls, these means of violence are designed to injure, kill, demolish and terrorize with maximum efficiency. Century by century, then decade by decade, and now year by year, this efficiency has grown as people and governments have applied talents and resources to that end.

The fact is, however, that it is not true that violence is the only effective means of action in crucial conflict situations. Throughout history, under a variety of political systems, people in every part of the world have waged conflict and wielded undeniable power by using a very different technique of struggle—one which does not kill and destroy. That technique is nonviolent action. Although it has been known by a variety of names, its basis has always been the same: the belief that the exercise of power depends on the consent of the ruled who, by withdrawing that consent, can control and even destroy the power of their opponent. In other words, nonviolent action is a technique used to control, combat and destroy the opponent's power by nonviolent means of wielding power. Although much effort has gone into increasing the efficiency of violent conflict, no comparable efforts have yet gone into making nonviolent action more effective and hence more likely to be substituted for violence.

And yet nonviolent action has already had a long history, which has remained largely unknown because historians have been so overwhelmingly concerned with other matters. In fact, there was until recently so little awareness of the tradition and history of nonviolent struggle that nonviolent actionists have, by and large, improvised their responses independently of past practice. This situation is only now beginning to change.

That there is a rich lode of material awaiting the analyst and actionist is abundantly clear. Even at the present early stage of investigation, he who looks can find numerous examples, ranging from ancient Rome to the civil rights struggle in the United States and the resistance of the Czechs and Slovaks to the Russian invasion of 1968. By searching diligently through scattered sources, he can find mention of plebeian protests against Rome as far back as the fifth century B.C.; he can trace the resistance of the Netherlands to Spanish rule in mid-sixteenth century Europe. But the history of nonviolent struggle in these centuries still remains to be written. What we have now are only brief glimpses.

In more modern times, however, the picture becomes more crowded. Important examples of nonviolent action and struggle occur in extremely varied settings. For example, to an extent which has on the whole been ignored, the American colonists used nonviolent resistance in their struggle against Britain, refusing to pay taxes and debts, refusing to import, refusing to obey laws they considered unjust, using independent political institutions, and severing social and economic contact with both the British and pro-British colonists.

Later, especially in the late nineteenth and early twentieth centuries, working people in many countries used noncooperation in the form of strikes and economic boycotts to improve conditions and to gain greater power. The Russian Revolution of 1905 is full of nonviolent responses to the events of "Bloody Sunday": paralyzing strikes, refusal to obey censorship regulations, establishment of "parallel" organs of government—these were only some of the pressures which led the Tsar's government to the promise of a more liberal governmental system. When the collapse of the tsarist system came in 1917 it was because it had disintegrated in face of an overwhelmingly nonviolent revolution—months before the Bolsheviks seized control in October. Nor does nonviolent pressure always have to be "against"; it can also be "for" as was made clear in Berlin in 1920, when the bureaucracy and population, who remained loyal to the existing Ebert government, brought down the militarist Kapp *Putsch* by refusing to cooperate with it.

Gandhi, who was the outstanding strategist of nonviolent action, regarded nonviolent struggle as a means of matching forces, one which had the greatest capacity for bringing real freedom and justice. The classic national Gandhian struggle was the 1930–31 campaign, which began with the famous Salt March as a prelude to civil disobedience against the British monopoly. A year-long nonviolent campaign followed. It shook British power in India and ended with negotiations between equals.

Despite highly unfavorable circumstances, nonviolent resistance sometimes also produced political tremors in certain Nazi-occupied countries during World War II. Occasionally—as in Norway—where Quisling's effort to set up a Corporative State was thwarted by nonviolent resistance—it won some battles. Covert noncooperation and, very rarely, nonviolent defiance even helped save the lives of Jews. During the same period, on the other side of the world, popular nonviolent action was being used successfully to dissolve the power of two Central American dictators. Communist systems, too, have felt the power of nonviolent action in the East German Rising in 1953, in strikes in Soviet prison camps, and in the nonviolent phase of the 1956 Hungarian Revolution. In the United States nonviolent action has played a major role in the struggles of Afro-Americans from the Montgomery bus boycott on. And in 1968, one of the most remarkable demonstrations of unprepared nonviolent resistance for national defense purposes took place in Czechoslovakia after the Russian invasion. The struggle was not successful, but the Czechs and Slovaks were able to hold out far longer—from August to April—than they could have with military resistance; even in defeat, it is a case meriting careful study. The achievements and victories of past nonviolent struggles, although often inadequate, have nevertheless frequently been remarkable, especially when one considers the usually small number of actual participants, and the general improvised, unprepared character of the resistance.

Another characteristic of nonviolent action is its great variety, in degree of success and in purpose and method. Sometimes nonviolent action may be used to achieve reforms or limited objectives (as in the Montgomery bus boycott); sometimes to destroy a whole regime (as in Russia in February-March 1917); sometimes to defend a government under attack (as in Czechoslovakia). Often deliberate efforts may be made to keep the struggle nonviolent, while in other cases nonviolence is not premeditated. Although the range of methods available in this type of struggle is vast, effective utilization of a considerable number of methods in the same case has taken place only rarely, as in the Russian revolutions. Only in a few cases (as in the Continental Association, the nonviolent "battle plan" of the First Continental Congress, and in India's 1930-31 campaign) has there been planned strategic phasing of the development of the struggle. Only once in a while—as with Gandhi—has there been conscious use of both strategic and tactical planning. Only rarely, as in Germany in the 1920s, during World War II in the case of governments-in-exile, and in Czechoslovakia in 1968, has there been official government backing for nonviolent resistance to usurpers. Many other variations in nonviolent action exist and will continue.

However, implicitly or explicitly, all nonviolent struggle has a basic assumption in common and that is its view of the nature of power and how to deal with it.

# 1

# The Nature
# and Control
# of Political Power

## INTRODUCTION

Unlike utopians, advocates of nonviolent action do not seek to "control" power by rejecting it or abolishing it. Instead, they recognize that power is inherent in practically all social and political relationships and that its control is "the basic problem in political theory" [1] and in political reality. They also see that it is necessary to wield power in order to control the power of threatening political groups or regimes. That assumption they share with advocates of violence, although they part company with them on many other points.

Social power may be briefly defined as the capacity to control the behavior of others, directly or indirectly, through action by groups of people, which action impinges on other groups of people. [2] Political power is that kind of social power which is wielded for political objectives, especially by governmental institutions or by people in opposition to or in support of such institutions. Political power thus refers to the total authority, influence, pressure and coercion which may be applied to achieve or prevent the implementation of the wishes of the power-holder.[3] In this book, when used alone, the term power is to be understood as referring to political power.

## WHAT IS THE BASIC NATURE OF POLITICAL POWER?

All types of struggle, and all means to control governments or to defend them against attack, are based upon certain basic assumptions about the nature of power. These are not usually explicit. In fact, so little do people stop to think about these assumptions that people are rarely aware of them and would often find it hard to articulate them. This is true of advocates of both nonviolent and violent action. Nevertheless, all responses to the "how" of dealing with an opponent's power are rooted in assumptions about the nature of power. An erroneous or inadequate view of the nature of political power is unlikely to produce satisfactory and effective action for dealing with it.

Basically, there appear to be two views of the nature of power. One can see people as dependent upon the good will, the decisions and the support of their government or of any other hierarchical system to which they belong. Or, conversely, one can see that government or system dependent on the people's good will, decisions and support. One can see the power of a government as emitted from the few who stand at the pinnacle of command. Or one can see that power, in all governments, as continually rising from many parts of the society. One can also see power as self-perpetuating, durable, not easily or quickly controlled or destroyed. Or political power can be viewed as fragile, always dependent for its strength and existence upon a replenishment of its sources by the cooperation of a multitude of institutions and people—cooperation which may or may not continue.

Nonviolent action is based on the second of these views: that governments depend on people, that power is pluralistic, and that political power is fragile because it depends on many groups for reinforcement of its power sources. The first view—that people depend on governments, that political power is monolithic, that it can really come from a few men, and that it is durable and self-perpetuating—appears to underlie most political violence. (A notable exception is guerrilla war in its predominently political stages.) The argument of this chapter is that the theory of power underlying nonviolent action is sounder and more accurate than the theory underlying most violent action, especially military struggle. In contrast to the pluralistic-dependency theory of nonviolent action—to which the bulk of this chapter is devoted—we might call this other view the "monolith theory."

The "monolith theory" of power assumes that the power of a government is a relatively fixed *quantum* (i.e. "a discrete unit quantity of energy"), a "given," a strong, independent, durable (if not indestructible), self-reinforcing, and self-perpetuating force. Because of these assumed characteristics, it follows that in open conflict such power cannot in the last analysis be controlled or destroyed simply by people but only by the threat or use of overwhelming physical might. The opponent's power may increase somewhat in the course of the struggle, or it may be somewhat reduced. But it is almost an axiom that in severe crises a hostile government's power can be significantly reduced, obstructed, or demolished only by destructive power—something like blasting chips or chunks off a solid stone block with explosives until it has been brought down to size or obliterated. War is based on this view of the nature of political power: faced with the actual or potential destruction of men, weapons, cities, industries, transport, communications and the like, the enemy will be forced to accept a settlement or to surrender (unless *he* has the greater destructive capacity). Nuclear weapons are the extreme development of the approach to control and combat based on this monolith view of the nature of political power.

If it were true that political power possesses the durability of a solid stone pyramid, then it would also be true that such power could only be controlled by the voluntary self-restraint of rulers (discussed below), by changes in the "ownership" of the monolith (the State)—whether with regular procedures (such as elections) or with irregular ones (regicide or *coup d'état)*, or by destructive violence (conventional war). The monolith view would not allow for the possibility of other types of effective pressure and control. But the monolith view of a government's power is quite inaccurate and ignores the nature of the power of any ruler or regime.

Nor can belief in the monolith theory by the rulers themselves make it come true. That theory can only alter reality when both the subjects and the opponents of a regime presenting this monolithic image of itself can be induced to believe the theory. Then, if the "owners" of the monolith refused to grant concessions, dissidents would either have to submit helplessly or resort only to the destructive attack called for by that theory of power. However, since the monolith theory is factually not true, and since *all* governments are dependent on the society they rule, even a regime which believes itself to be a monolith, and *appears* to be one, can be weakened and shattered by the undermining and severance of its sources of power, when people act upon the theory of power presented in this chapter.

If the monolith theory is not valid, but nevertheless forms the basic assumption of modern war and other types of control, the resulting underlying fallacy helps to explain why war and other controls have suffered from disadvantages and limitations. Relying on destructive violence to control political power is regarded by theorists of nonviolent action as being just as irrational as attempting to use a lid to control steam from a caldron, while allowing the fire under it to blaze uncontrolled.

Nonviolent action is based on the view that political power can most efficiently be controlled *at its sources*. This chapter is an exploration of why and how this may be done. It will lead us to basic questions concerning the roots of political power and the nature of government. It will finally lead us to the distinctive way of looking at the problem of how to control power on which nonviolent action rests. This conceptual framework is both old and new.[4] It is rooted in the insights of some of the most respected political thinkers concerned with the nature of society and politics.

## SOCIAL ROOTS OF POLITICAL POWER

An error frequently made by students of politics is to view political decisions, events and problems in isolation from the society in which they exist.[5] If they are studied within their social context, however, it may be found that the roots of political power reach beyond and below the formal structure of the State into the society itself. If this is so, it will follow that the nature of the means of controlling power will differ radically from those most suitable if it were not true.

It is an obvious, simple, but often forgotten observation of great theoretical and practical significance that the power wielded by individuals and groups in highest positions of command and decision in any government —whom we shall for brevity call "rulers"[6]—is not intrinsic to them. Such power must come from outside them. True, some men have greater personal qualities or greater intelligence, or inspire greater confidence than others, but this in no way refutes the fact that the political power which they wield as rulers comes from the society which they govern. Thus if a ruler is to wield power, he must be able to direct the behavior of other people, draw on large resources, human and material, wield an apparatus of coercion, and direct a bureaucracy in the administration of his policies. All these components of political power are external to the person of the power-holder.

The situation is essentially that described by the sixteenth-century

French writer Étienne de La Boétie, in speaking of the power of a tyrant: "He who abuses you so has only two eyes, has but two hands, one body, and has naught but what has the least man of the great and infinite number of your cities, except for the advantage you give him to destroy you."[7] Auguste Comte also argued in the early nineteenth century that the then popular theory was not correct in attributing to rulers a permanent, unchanging degree of power. On the contrary, while granting the influence of the political system on the society as a whole, Comte insisted that the power of a ruler was variable and that it depended on the degree to which the society granted him that power.[8] Other, more recent writers have made the same point.[9]

## A. Sources of power

If political power is not intrinsic to the power-holder, it follows that it must have outside sources. In fact, political power appears to emerge from the interaction of all or several of the following sources:

**1. Authority**   The extent and intensity of the ruler's authority among the subjects is a crucial factor affecting the ruler's power.

Authority may be defined as the ". . . right to command and direct, to be heard or obeyed by others,"[10] voluntarily accepted by the people and therefore existing without the imposition of sanctions. The possessor of authority may not actually be superior; it is enough that he be perceived and accepted as superior. While not identical with power, authority is nevertheless clearly a main source of power.

**2. Human resources**   A ruler's power is affected by the number of persons who obey him, cooperate with him, or provide him with special assistance, as well as by the proportion of such persons in the general population, and the extent and forms of their organizations.

**3. Skills and knowledge**   The ruler's power is also affected by the skills, knowledge and abilities of such persons, and the relation of their skills, knowledge and abilities to his needs.

**4. Intangible factors**   Psychological and ideological factors, such as habits and attitudes toward obedience and submission, and the presence or absence of a common faith, ideology, or sense of mission, all affect the power of the ruler in relation to the people.

**5. Material resources**   The degree to which the ruler controls property, natural resources, financial resources, the economic system, means of communication and transportation helps to determine the limits of his power.

**6. Sanctions**    The final source of a ruler's power is the type and extent of sanctions at his disposal, both for use against his own subjects and in conflicts with other rulers.

As John Austin wrote, sanctions are "an enforcement of obedience,"[11] used by rulers against their subjects to supplement voluntary acceptance of their authority and to increase the degree of obedience to their commands. They may be violent or not; they may be intended as punishment or as deterrence. Citizens may sometimes apply sanctions against their governments or against each other (these will be discussed below). Still other sanctions may be applied by governments against other governments and may take a variety of forms, such as the breaking of diplomatic relations, economic embargoes, military invasions and bombings. Violent domestic sanctions, such as imprisonment or execution, are commonly intended to punish disobedience, not to achieve the objective of the original command, except insofar as such sanctions may inhibit future disobedience by other persons. Other violent sanctions sometimes, and most nonviolent sanctions usually, are intended to achieve the original objective; this is often the case in conventional war, strikes, political noncooperation and boycotts. Sanctions are usually a key element in domestic and international politics.

It is always a matter of the *degree* to which some or all of these sources of power are present; only rarely, if ever, are all of them completely available to a ruler or completely absent. But their availability is subject to constant variation, which brings about an increase or decrease in the ruler's power. Baron de Montesquieu observed that "those who govern have a power which, in some measure, has need of fresh vigor every day . . ."[12] To the degree that the sources of power are available without limitation, the ruler's power is unlimited. However, the opposite is also true: to the degree that the availability of these sources is limited, the ruler's political power is also limited.[13]

**B. These sources depend on obedience**

A closer examination of the sources of the ruler's power will indicate that they depend *intimately* upon the obedience and cooperation of the subjects. Let us, for example, consider *authority* from this point of view. Authority is necessary for the existence and operation of any regime.[14] No matter how great their means of physical coercion, all rulers require an acceptance of their authority, their right to rule and to command.[15] The key to habitual obedience is to reach the mind.[16] Thomas Hill Green points out that "obedience will scarcely be habitual unless it is loyal, not forced."[17] Because authority must by definition be voluntarily accepted by the people, the authority of the ruler will depend upon the goodwill of the subjects and will vary as that goodwill varies.

If a ruler's need for acceptance of his authority is basic, loss of authority will have serious consequences for his position and power. Just as subjects may accept a ruler's authority because they believe it is merited on grounds of morality and of the well-being of their society or country, subjects may for the same reasons at times deny the ruler's claims to authority over them. The weakening or collapse of that authority inevitably tends to loosen the subjects' predisposition toward obedience. Obedience will no longer be habitual; the decision to obey or not to obey will be made consciously, and obedience may be refused.

If the subjects deny the ruler's right to rule and to command, they are withdrawing the general agreement, or group consent, which makes possible the existing government.[18] This loss of authority sets in motion the disintegration of the ruler's power.[19] That power is reduced to the degree that he is denied authority. Where the loss is extreme, the existence of that particular government is threatened.

A second point to be considered is *the contribution of the subjects to the established system*. Clearly, every ruler must depend upon the cooperation and assistance of his subjects in operating the economic and administrative system. Every ruler needs the skill, knowledge, advice, labor and administrative ability of a significant portion of his subjects. The more extensive and detailed the ruler's control is, the more such assistance he will require. These contributions to the ruler's power will range, for example, from the specialized knowledge of a technical expert, the research endeavors of a scientist, and the organizational abilities of a department head to the assistance of typists, factory workers, transportation workers, and farmers. Both the economic and the political systems operate because of the contributions of many people, individuals, organizations and subgroups.

The ruler's power depends on the continual availability of all this assistance, not only from individual members, officials, employees and the like,[20] but from the subsidiary organizations and institutions which compose the system as a whole. These may be departments, bureaus, branches, committees and the like. Just as individuals and independent groups may refuse to cooperate, so too these unit organizations may refuse to provide sufficient help to maintain effectively the ruler's position and to enable him to implement his policies.[21] "Thus no complex can carry out a superior order if its members (either unit organizations or individuals) will not enable it to do so . . ." [22]

If the multitude of "assistants" reject the ruler's authority, they may then carry out his wishes inefficiently, or may take unto themselves certain decisions, or may even flatly refuse to continue their usual assistance.[23] In efforts to ensure the desired degree of assistance and cooperation, sanctions may, of course, be applied. But because rulers need more than grudging, outward forms of compliance by this multitude of subjects, efforts to obtain this assistance by compulsion will inevitably be inadequate as long as the extent and intensity of the ruler's authority among these subjects is limited.[24]

Because, then, of dependence on other people to operate the system, the ruler is continually subject to influence and restriction by both his direct assistants and the general populace. This control will be greatest where his dependence is greatest.

It remains to discuss the relation between *sanctions* and submission. If, in the face of serious unrest, the regime does not make changes to meet popular demands, increased reliance will have to be placed on enforcement. Such sanctions are usually possible despite dissatisfaction with the regime because very often while one section of the populace rejects the ruler's authority another section remains loyal and willing to help the regime to maintain itself and carry out its policies. In such a case a ruler may use the loyal subjects as police or soldiers to inflict sanctions on the remainder of the people.[25] However, sanctions, even in such a case, will not be the determining force in maintaining the regime—for several reasons. The ruling group (foreign or domestic) will itself still be united by something other than sanctions.[26] Furthermore, any ruler's ability to apply sanctions at home or abroad arises from and depends upon a significant degree of help from the subjects themselves.

Sanctions *are* important in maintaining a ruler's political power—especially in crises. But *the ability to impose sanctions* itself derives from the obedience and cooperation of at least some subjects; also, *whether those sanctions are effective* depends on the subjects' particular pattern of submission. Let us discuss each of these.

Without various types of cooperation and assistance, no ruler could impose sanctions, either on the people he wishes to rule in his own country, or internationally on foreign enemies. This ability depends to a considerable degree on whether his subjects are willing to become police and soldiers for him, and if so, upon the degree of efficiency with which they carry out commands to impose sanctions.[27] Furthermore, the material weapons themselves are social products. Once one gets much beyond bows and arrows, the manufacturing process for weapons—guns, bombs, planes, tanks and so on—depends on social cooperation, often of many people and of diverse organizations and institutions. Even technology has not changed this. New developments in communications and weaponry may in the future reduce the extent of assistance needed at a given moment to inflict sanctions, and may change the types of sanctions. The relationship of dependency will not be reduced or abolished, however.

Finally, the effectiveness of even enthusiastic police and troops in carrying out their tasks is often highly influenced by the degree to which the general population gives them voluntary support or obstructs their efforts.[28] As W.A. Rudlin points out, it is not that the State rests on "force," but that the State possesses "force" as long as most of its subjects deem this desirable.[29] Therefore, the capacity to *impose* sanctions rests on cooperation. But the *effectiveness* or ineffectiveness of sanctions when available and used also depends on the response of the subjects against whom they are threatened or applied.

Thus, the compliance pattern of the subjects will largely determine the extent to which sanctions are "required" to bolster obedience and even their relative effectiveness when used. We are speaking here of the degree to which people obey without threats, and the degree to which they continue to disobey despite punishment. Speaking of the general pattern of obedience under "normal" conditions, Karl W. Deutsch has argued that the chances of detection and punishment, even when small, help to strengthen and reinforce the pattern of obedience. This general obedience is sufficiently widespread and strong to make enforcement practical and probable in the minority of cases of disobedience. Enforcement and obedience are, then, interdependent: the greater the voluntary obedience, the greater the chances of detection and punishment of deviations.[30] Compliance and enforcement thus reinforce each other: the stronger the compliance pattern, the more effective the enforcement (and conversely). Also the weaker the compliance pattern, the less effective the enforcement (and conversely), with a continual range of variations. This applies to all types of regimes, including totalitarian systems.[31]

The ruler's power, we may summarize from the above discussion, is therefore not a static "given" *quantum*. Instead, his power varies because the number, type and quality of the social forces he controls varies. "The internal stability of a regime can be measured by the ratio between the number and strength of the social forces that it controls or conciliates, in a word, represents, and the number and strength of the social forces that it fails to represent and has against it."[32]

Similarly, the variations in the ruler's power are in turn directly or indirectly associated with the willingness of the subjects to accept the ruler, to obey, to cooperate with him and to carry out his wishes.[33] So important is the cooperation of the subjects in determining the availability of the sources of power, and hence the extent and capability of any ruler's power, that Bertrand de Jouvenel has put the ruler's political power, the sources of his power and the obedience of the subjects on an almost mathematical basis of equality.[34]

## WHY DO MEN OBEY?

The most important single quality of any government, without which it would not exist, must be the obedience and submission of its subjects. Obedience is at the heart of political power. The relationships between the ruler and the subjects, and the ancient question of why some men obey other men, therefore become relevant to our analysis.

Many people often assume that the issuance of a command and its execution form a single, more or less automatic operation and therefore that the wielding of political power is an entirely one-way relationship. If this were true, any suggestion that a ruler's power might be controlled by reducing and withdrawing obedience and cooperation would be absurd, for the command and its implementation would be inseparable. However, such an assumption is not true: the relationship between command and obedience is always one of mutual influence and some degree of inter-action—which is "mutually determined" action[35] involving a two-sided relationship between the ruler and the subjects.

Sanctions for disobedience are more severe in the relationship between ruler and subject than is usual in other relationships between persons who are superior in rank (superordinates) and those who are under the controls or orders of a superior (subordinates).[36] Nevertheless, certain basic similarities of interaction and dependence do exist between the ruler-subject relationship and all other superordinate-subordinate relationships. Professor Harold Lasswell, the German sociologist Georg Simmel and Chester I. Barnard, the American analyst of *The Functions of the Executive,* have all offered insights into the nature of this interaction and dependence. Professor Lasswell has described this mutual influence as "cue-giving" and "cue-taking."[37] He cites the orchestra as an example, observing that just as a conductor may impose penalties upon members who fail to follow his cues, so the orchestra if dissatisfied with the conductor can impose penalties and "by deliberate noncooperation or hostile agitation . . . may get him fired."[38] Lasswell adds that without the expected conformity by the subordinates (whether in the form of "passive acquiescence or active consent") the power relationship is not complete, despite the threat or infliction of sanctions.[39]

Simmel has offered other examples of interaction, which occur even where least expected.[40] He cites the relationship between the speaker and his audience, the teacher and his class, and the journalist and his readers as instances in which the subordinates actually influence the superordinate in a major way. "Thus, a highly complex interaction . . . is hidden here beneath the semblance of pure superiority of the one element and a purely passive being-led of the other."[41] Even in the case of certain types of personal relationships in which the exclusive function of one person is to serve the other, he says, and even in the case of the relation between the hypnotist and the hypnotized, an element of reciprocity and mutual dependence is involved. As he puts it, ". . . appearance shows an absolute influence, on the one side, and an absolute being-influenced, on the other; but it conceals an interaction, an exchange of influences . . ."[42] He concludes that ". . . even the most miserable slave . . . in some fashion at least, can still in this sense react to his master."[43]

Barnard has also pointed out that the same type of interaction takes place *between institutions* and between the various units *within a complex organization.*[44] Because the superordinate body is dependent on its subordinate members or suborganizations to carry out orders and tasks, he describes their operation as a "cooperative effort."[45]

The same type of interaction takes place in the State: commands and orders are not automatically obeyed. This is true in the relationship between ruler and subjects, between ruler and the regime's various departments and agencies, among the various departments, and, within each of them, between its head and its subordinate members.[46] The power relationship exists only when completed by the subordinates' obedience to the ruler's commands and compliance with his wishes. As we shall see, this does not always take place. Even where political power is backed by sanctions, some degree of interaction *always* exists between the rulers or superiors-in-rank and those to whom they give orders and commands.[47] The wielding of political power is *not,* therefore, a one-way process in which the ruler issues commands which are inevitably carried out. "Since political power is the control of other men," Franz

Neumann wrote, "political power . . . is always a two-sided relationship." [48] Furthermore, the interaction between ruler and subject takes place within a political and social setting in which a variety of factors may influence its course and outcome.

The variables in this interaction are generally three: the ruler (or leader), the subject (or follower), and the situation.[49] All are subject to constant mutual influence, changes in one altering the reactions of the other two, and in turn requiring a new response from the original factor. The degree to which the ruler succeeds in wielding power and achieving his objectives thus depends upon the degree of obedience and cooperation emerging from this interaction. Both domestically and internationally a regime's power "is in proportion to its ability to make itself obeyed and win from that obedience the means of action. It all turns on that obedience. Who knows the reasons for that obedience knows the inner nature of Power." [50]

Having established the fact that obedience is necessary if the command is to be carried out and also the fact that obedience is not inevitable, we come to the ancient question: why do the many obey the few?

How is it that a ruler is able to obtain and maintain political domination over the multitude of his subjects? Why do they in such large numbers submit to him and obey him,[51] even when it is clearly not in their interest to do so? How is it that a ruler may even use his subjects for ends which are contrary to the subjects' own interests?[52] All these questions are not new. But in asking them here as though they were new, we may rediscover old insights and explore afresh their implications. The answers will be important in determining what solutions are to be offered to the problem of how to control political power. As the sociologists Hans Gerth and C. Wright Mills have concluded, ". . . from a psychological point of view the crux of the problem of power rests in understanding the origin, constitution, and maintainance of voluntary obedience." [53]

Thomas Hobbes' answer in the seventeenth century to the question of obedience was simple. Subjects obey their rulers because of fear, he wrote, either fear of the ruler himself or of one another.[54] Were fear the only reason for obedience there would be only two possible means of control of the sovereign's power: either inducing in the ruler self-imposed limitations, or threatening or using superior fear-instilling power. Today these means are often seen to be inadequate. Their inadequacy may be rooted in an erroneous or incomplete understanding of the reasons for obedience. Hobbes' view, taken by itself, is not true. Other factors in addition to fear have played a significant role in the development of governments and the maintenance of obedience. It is necessary to look beyond Hobbes' conceptual framework to discover the reasons for obedience.

## A. The reasons are various and multiple

Actually there is no single self-sufficient explanation for obedience to rulers. Nor can political obedience be explained solely in rational terms. The reasons are multiple, complex and interrelated; different combinations and proportions of reasons produce obedience in various situations. A number of specific answers and explanations have, however, been offered. We can learn much from them, provided we remember that no one answer can be totally adequate, and that each must be seen in the perspective of the others.

**1. Habit**      One reason why men obey is that obedience has long been the practice of humanity, and it has become a habit. In the opinion of some, the habit of obedience is in fact "the essential reason" for continued obedience.[55] David Hume said that habit consolidates what other principles of human nature have imperfectly founded. Once accustomed to obedience, he wrote, men "never think of departing from that path in which they and their ancestors have constantly trod, and to which they are confined by so many urgent and visible motives." [56]

No one claims, however, that habit is the sole cause of obedience. Convincing reasons felt over a long period are necessary to make obedience habitual. Such obedience, Austin suggested, is the consequence of a combination of various factors such as custom, prejudice, utility, and a perception of the expediency of political government.[57] Further, in times of political crisis, or when the demands of the ruler increase sharply, habit ceases to be a complete explanation of obedience.[58] Unless other adequate reasons for obedience also exist, it may then cease.

**2. Fear of sanctions**      The fear of sanctions has been widely acknowledged as a source of obedience.[59] While sanctions may take various forms, such as social and economic pressures, we are here largely concerned with the sanctions provided in the law and practice of the State. These generally involve the threat or use of some form of physical violence against the disobedient subject, and induce obedience by ". . . power merely coercive, a power really operating on people simply through their fears . . ."[60]

The intent behind such sanctions may be both to provide a punishment or reprisal for failure to meet an obligation (thus, sanctions applied against subjects are usually not primarily intended to achieve the objective of the original command) and also to encourage the continued compliance of *other* subjects by inspiring in them, through exemplary cases, a fear of the sanctions for disobedience.[61] Fear of violent internal sanctions against individuals and the existence of means for waging violent conflict against groups (both internally and externally) have often been regarded as important in the origin of the State and of political obedience.[62] The role of fear of sanctions is especially important when other reasons for obedience have become weakened. Yet political power cannot be reduced simply to physical might, and fear of sanctions in support of laws and commands is not the sole reason for obedience.

**3. Moral obligation**     A third reason for obedience is that subjects feel a moral obligation to obey. This is distinct from a legal obligation to do so, although certain types of moral obligation may be associated with a legal obligation. A sense among the subjects of a moral obligation to obey is a common quality of all forms of political organization.[63]

A sense of moral obligation to obey is partly a product of the normal process by which the individual absorbs the customs, ways and beliefs of his society as he grows up,[64] and partly the result of deliberate indoctrination.[65] The line between these processes is not .always clear. They produce in the subject an inner "constraining power"[66] which leads him to obedience and submission.[67] This sense of moral obligation may not originate with the ruler but, instead, come from general views about the welfare of the whole society or from religious principles. On the other hand, because of the limited effectiveness of fear, rulers may try to influence "the most efficacious of all" restraints, that of "a man's own conscience."[68] The ruler's "secret of success" then becomes the subject's mind, and propaganda becomes "the indispensable adjunct of the police."[69]

The origins and effects of such feelings vary, but generally they may arise from four considerations:[70]

a) The common good of society. Belief that constraint by government is for the common good is always an element in political obedience.[71] Hume described this as the motive which first produced submission and obedience to governments and one which continued to do so.[72] Obedience makes protection from antisocial persons possible,[73] and promotes the good of all. As T.H. Green put it, both morality and political subjection originate in general rational recognition of "a common well-being," embodied in rules to restrain those who would violate it.[74] This view includes both belief in the benefits of government in general and of a particular government as compared to any possible alternative.[75]

Belief that political obedience is for the common good—held by both the general population and those able to impose sanctions for disobedience—thus "gives great security to any government."[76] Without this belief, says Green, no one would recognize any claim to the common obedience of the subjects.[77]

The degree to which the law or the particular regime is identified with the common good will help to determine the degree of loyal obedience.[78] However, a considerable discrepancy may be tolerated, for belief in the advantages of government makes people averse to resistance and displeased when others resist.[79] Although dissatisfied, people may therefore continue to obey for fear that resistance might entail still greater evil and that government itself might collapse.[80]

b) Suprahuman factors. A second source of moral obligation leading to political obedience lies in the identification of the lawgiver or ruler with suprahuman qualities, powers, or principles which make disobedience inconceivable. These qualities may originate in magic, supernatural beings, deities, or "true-believer" ideologies (both political and religious). But the effect on obedience is similar. The ruling system thus takes on the character of a religious or nonreligious "theocracy"—a development which significantly contributes to obedience,[81] for disobedience then becomes heresy, impiety, a betrayal of race, nation, or class, or a defiance of the gods,[82] of History, or of Truth. Various methods, such as rituals, may be used to keep alive deference and belief in the particular suprahuman qualities, powers, or principles identified with the lawgiver or ruler.

c) Legitimacy of the command. Commands are also obeyed because they are considered legitimate owing to their source[83] and their issuer.[84] If the command is given by someone in an accepted official position, if it is seen as being in accordance with tradition, established law and constitution, if the ruler has obtained his position through the established procedure, then the subject will usually feel a greater obligation to obey than he would if these conditions were not present.[85] More rarely, by contrast, in revolutionary situations legitimacy may derive not from tradition but from "the people," "the revolution," and activities during the struggle against the previous, now "illegitimate," ruler or system. There are also other sources of legitimacy[86] which contribute to obedience by increasing the ruler's authority.

d) Conformity of commands to accepted norms. The fourth source of feelings of moral obligation to obey rulers lies in the conformity of their commands to accept norms of conduct. People then obey because the behavior commanded by the ruler is what they believe to be right in any case, such as not stealing or not killing. The law is then obeyed because of the "rationality of its contents."[87] As Green puts it, the law corresponds to the "general sense of what is equitable and necessary."[88]

**4. Self-interest**    Nonpolitical organizations and institutions—business, educational, scientific and the like—often obtain the desired cooperation of individuals by offering incentives, such as money, position and prestige. Similarly, incentives may also be important in political institutions, including the State, as they help to procure the obedience, cooperation and active assistance of subjects. Hume lists self-interest as a secondary, supporting, reason for obedience which operates in combination with other reasons.[89] People who dislike a ruler or system may nevertheless continue not only to obey passively, but even to serve actively in what they consider to be their own positive self-interest. There may also be a negative type of self-interest, involving the avoidance of molestation and inconvenience; this is related to sanctions and is discussed under that topic.

Positive self-interest is most important if the ruler is to obtain the various types of assistants and helpers he needs to run the government and to rule. Once the ruler is established, he is able to encourage the expectation of rewards.[90] Normally his ministers and military force, for example, "find an immediate and visible interest in supporting his authority."[91] Such self-interest may also be especially important for persons who occupy secondary governmental positions in administration, enforcement and the like, as well as nongovernmental intermediary positions in the society.

Self-interest may be appealed to in terms of: *prestige* (the hope for titles, decorations and various honors); *relative power position* (maintenance and improvement of one's status in the political and social pyramid);[92] or *direct or indirect financial gain* ("every man is supposed to have his price").[93] These rewards especially help the ruler to obtain the services of the minority, which he will use to rule and control the majority.[94]

While direct economic rewards have generally been limited to relatively small numbers of persons, economic self-interest may now in certain societies be an increasingly important motive for obedience among a larger percentage of the population. With the multiplication of government jobs and controls over the economy, more people may find it to their interest to remain loyal, to obey, and to cooperate. Also, indirect economic rewards may encourage general submission; higher standards of living and increasing material benefits in highly industrialized countries may contribute significantly to continuing political obedience and positive assistance for the system and regime.

**5. Psychological identification with the ruler**   Subjects may also obey and cooperate because they have a close emotional identification with the ruler or with the regime or system. This identification may be stronger and more usual in societies in which the common beliefs and sense of purpose have broken down; people often need something or someone to believe in and some source of purpose and direction in their lives. Deutsch refers to persons who look "upon the government in some manner as an extension of themselves or upon themselves as an extension of the government . . . the triumphs and successes of the government are felt as personal triumphs by its subjects; its defeats are experienced as personal dishonor or misfortune . . ."[95] This phenomenon is not limited to any particular political system.

**6. Zones of indifference**   Although subjects do not obey all laws with equal thoroughness or enthusiasm, it does not follow that all those laws which do not arouse enthusiastic obedience will be poorly obeyed in the absence of threats of sanctions. This is because, in Robert M. MacIver's words, "there is a margin of indifference and a margin of tolerance."[96] Barnard also observes that one reason that it is possible to achieve enduring cooperation is the existence of " 'a zone of indifference' within which each individual will accept orders without consciously questioning their authority . . ."[97] How wide this zone is will vary, depending on a number of social and political conditions and the inducements offered for obedience.

**7. Absence of self-confidence among subjects**   Many people do not have sufficient confidence in themselves, their judgment and their capacities to make them capable of disobedience and resistance. Having no strong will of their own, they accept that of their rulers, and sometimes prefer rulers who will direct their lives and relieve them of the task of making decisions. The subjects may be disillusioned, exhausted, apathetic, or possessed of inertia, or they may lack a belief system which makes it possible both to evaluate when one ought to obey and disobey, and also to give confidence in one's right and ability to make such a decision. Lack of self-confidence may also be influenced by a belief that the ruling group is more qualified to make decisions and to carry them out than are the subjects. This attitude may be based on perceived greater competence,[98] social customs and class distinctions,[99] or conscious indoctrination.[100]

One consequence of the lack of self-confidence is a tendency to avoid responsibility, to seek to delegate it upward and to attribute greater authority to superiors in the hierarchy than is in fact merited.[101] People lacking self-confidence may seek a ruler, a leader, a despot, a tyrant who will relieve them of responsibility for guiding their present and their future.[102] Wrote Rousseau: "Slaves lose everything in their chains, even the desire of escaping from them: they love their servitude, as the comrades of Ulysses loved their brutish condition."[103] Even where subjects wish to alter the established order, they may remain submissive because they lack confidence in their ability to act effectively in bringing about the desired changes. As long as people lack self-confidence they are unlikely to do anything other than obey, cooperate with, and submit to their rulers.

## B. Obtaining the ruler's functionaries and agents

Every ruler uses the obedience and cooperation he receives from *part* of the society to rule the *whole*. He is assisted by a "veritable army of underlings,"[104] a complex graded organization of subordinates, functionaries and agents,[105] who help to subject the society as a whole to his domination.[106] This requires and produces a hierarchical system.[107] Because of the key role of this section of the population, brief special attention to their motives for obedience and cooperation is required. As with the general populace, these motives are various and multiple: habit, fear of sanctions, moral obligation, self-interest, identification with the ruler, indifference within very broad limits to particular policies, and insufficient self-confidence to refuse. While the preceding discussion of these motives also applies here, it seems that for this group a particular motive may be of either more or less importance than among the general population. Feelings of moral obligation to obey and to provide help may be especially important. Within the ruling group, which includes this organization of functionaries and agents, "some common sentiment," "something like voluntary consent" is needed.[108] As already noted, self-interest may play a disproportionately large role; Boétie observed that there may be "as many people to whom tyranny seems profitable, as those to whom liberty would be agreeable."[109] Today, many people have vested interests in the continuance of established regimes and therefore continue to serve them.

Fear of sanctions is probably less important among the functionaries and agents than among the general populace. (An exception might be soldiers who are drafted into the army against their wishes and face severe sanctions should they mutiny.) Generally, however, violent sanctions are not decisive in obtaining the special assistance of functionaries and agents; other motives predominate. This may be important in getting them to refuse to assist groups which have illegally seized the State apparatus by a *coup d'état,* for example.

### C. Obedience is not inevitable[110]

Obedience to a ruler's command, though usual, is not inevitable. It always varies in degree with the individual concerned and with the social and political situation. Obedience is never universally practiced by the whole population. Many people sometimes disobey the law. Some people do so frequently. The degree of general compliance varies widely. The most powerful ruler receives no more than the habitual obedience of the bulk of the subjects.[111] Publicized cases of mass disobedience, defiance and noncooperation are simply more extensive dramatic evidences of this general truth. They are demonstrations that the wielding of political power is indeed a case of interaction.

People are generally law-abiding, except when "unmoored by catastophic events or by social convulsions."[112] At any given point in a given society there are limits within which a ruler must stay if his commands are to be obeyed. These limits are subject to change throughout the history of a society.[113] To the degree that the law and the ruler's general policies agree with the needs of a society and the general sense of what is desirable and tolerable, obedience will be widespread. But, Rudlin observed, "Obedience can be enforced only while the mass of men are in some sort of agreement with the law. There is no lack of examples of opposition and successful opposition, to government decision."[114]

It follows that under certain conditions subjects may be willing to put up with inconvenience, suffering and disruption of their lives rather than continue to submit passively or to obey a ruler whose policies they can no longer tolerate. Having long been accustomed to receiving widespread obedience, rulers do not always anticipate these eventualities.[115]

# THE ROLE OF CONSENT

In light of the above discussion, it is reasonable to view the political obedience on which a ruler's power is ultimately dependent as a consequence of a combination of a fear of sanctions and free consent—the latter arising either from a more or less nonrational acceptance of the standards and ways of one's society, or from a more or less rational consideration of the merits of the regime and the reasons for obeying it. This is compatible with discussions by several theorists who describe obedience as arising from a mixture of "coercion" and "consent."[116] Clearly sanctions *alone* could not produce the necessary degree, extent and constancy of obedience. Yet if *other* reasons for obedience are present, an increase in sanctions may increase compliance.[117] Nevertheless, the fact remains that sanctions do not *always* produce an increase in obedience. This may be because in order to produce obedience, sanctions must also operate through the volition, or will, of the subject. This possibility merits further exploration. If true, it has important political implications.

Let us first admit that there is a meaningful sense in which obedience is *not* voluntary, in which the individual is a more or less helpless victim of vast social and political forces which impinge upon him—even determining his beliefs, his moral standards, his attitudes to social and political events, and consequently his obedience to the State. If these forces are insufficient to produce obedience, there is always the repressive power of the State, which he has learned to fear. This combination of pressures, controls and repression is, more often than not, seen as a conclusive reason for the view that obedience follows more or less automatically from the issuance of commands. As we have seen, however, the wielding of political power involves social interaction, and obedience is by no means as uniform or universal as this deterministic view of obedience would lead us to expect. The reason for this inconsistency may be simple: the view that political obedience is constant, that it is determined by these social and political forces (or, if all else fails, will at least be produced by sanctions) is fallacious.

## A. Obedience is essentially voluntary

In reviewing the reasons for obedience we find that although they are highly influenced by various social forces, each reason must operate through the will or the opinion of the individual subject to be effective. If he is to obey, the subject must accept a combination of the current reasons for obeying as in fact being sufficient for obedience. Because sanctions do not automatically produce obedience, the subject's evaluation of the reasons for obedience will even include sanctions. The will or opinion of the individual is not constant and may change in response to new influences, events and forces. In varying degrees the individual's own will may then play an active role in the situation. There is thus an important sense in which the obedience of subjects is essentially the result of an act of volition.[118]

Even in the case of obedience by habit, the subject accepts the view that it is best to continue to obey without consciously trying to examine

why he should do so. Feelings of moral obligation, a psychological identification with the ruler, and acceptance of a "zone of indifference" all
involve a basically voluntary acceptance of the ruler's wishes. The role of
self-interest in procuring obedience may vary, depending upon the relative
importance given (more or less consciously) to it by the subject, in the
context of a variety of other attitudes. In certain situations the subject
may even conclude that it is in his self-interest to *disobey* a regime—
especially if he foresees its collapse. The degree of his lack of self-confidence also varies and may be influenced by changes in the attitudes of
other subjects.

Even in the case of sanctions, there is a role for an act of will, for
choice. The sanction must be *feared* and its consequences be seen as more
undesirable than the consequences of obedience. This is not to deny that
there is always "a margin of obedience which is won only by the use of
force or the threat of force."[119] Even Gandhi would admit that "consent is often forcibly procured by the despot."[120] To say there is a
role for will or choice even in the case of sanctions is to say that one can
choose to obey, thus avoiding the sanctions threatened for disobedience.
Or one can choose to disobey and risk receiving the threatened sanctions.

Here a distinction must be made between obedience and coercion by
direct physical violation. If, for example, a man who is ordered to go to
prison refuses to do so and is physically dragged there (that is, if he is
coerced by direct physical violation), he cannot be said to obey, argued
Austin. But if he *walks* to prison under a command backed by *threat*
of a sanction, then he in fact obeys and consents to the act, although he
may not approve of the command.[121] *Obedience thus exists only when
one has complied with or submitted to the command.*

Physical compulsion affecting only the body therefore does not obtain
*obedience.* Only certain types of objectives can be achieved by direct physical compulsion of disobedient subjects—such as moving them physically,
preventing them from moving physically, or seizing their money or property. Even to achieve such limited objectives in the face of a larger number of disobedient subjects would require a vast number of enforcement
agents able to force or constrain each of them physically. Most other objectives of commands, and certainly active cooperation, cannot be produced
by even continuous direct physical violation of persons—whether the command is to dig a ditch, obey traffic signals, work in a factory, offer technical advice, or arrest political opponents. The overwhelming percentage
of a ruler's commands and objectives can only be achieved by inducing
the subject to be *willing* for some reason to carry them out. Punishment

of one who disobeys a command does not achieve the objective (for example, the ditch remains undug even if the men who refused to dig it have been shot).

The threat of physical compulsion or sanctions produces obedience and consent only when the threat affects the subject's mind and emotions —in other words, when the subject fears the sanctions and is unwilling to suffer them. This was Simmel's point too: he argued that despite penalties for disobedience, the choice to obey or to disobey is always possible.[122] *It is not the sanctions themselves which produce obedience but the fear of them.*[123] In Robert Michels' words: "Even when authority rests on mere physical coercion it is accepted by those ruled, although the acceptance may be due to a fear of force."[124] Of course, it is almost axiomatic that most people in most situations are quite unwilling to suffer the penalties for disobedience. Even when their dislike of the status quo is high, there will be hesitation. Gandhi, for example, on the basis of his efforts to produce large-scale disobedience and voluntary acceptance of imposed sanctions, observed that feelings must be very intense to make possible the acceptance of such sacrifice.[125] However, disobedience sometimes occurs despite sanctions, as will be described later in more detail.

If, then, choice and volition are present even where obedience is largely produced by sanctions—where one could least expect an act of will —the obedience of subjects in general can be regarded as voluntary and as arising from consent. This is especially so because generally people obey for reasons other than the threat of sanctions. Clearly, permanent obedience cannot be produced only by threat of sanctions.[126] It is reasonable to conclude with Austin that obedient subjects *will* the obedience they render, that they obey because of some motive, that they consent to obey. Their obedience is therefore essentially voluntary.[127] This is one of the significant characteristics of government.

The conclusions of the discussion thus far may be put succinctly. A ruler's power is dependent upon the availability of its several sources. This availability is determined by the degree of obedience and cooperation given by the subjects. Such obedience and cooperation are, however, not inevitable, and despite inducements, pressures, and even sanctions, obedience remains essentially voluntary. Therefore, *all government is based upon consent.*[128]

Support for this view comes from widely diverse political thinkers and actionists. For example, Austin wrote that the view "that every government continues through the people's consent" simply means that in every society "the people are determined by motives of some description or another, to obey their government habitually . . ."[129] William Godwin, an earlier and more libertarian thinker, argued that people can be held in subjection only insofar as ". . . they are willing to be subject. All government is founded in opinion."[130] Acceptance of this view came even from Adolf Hitler: "For, in the long run, government systems are not held together by the pressure of force, but rather by the belief in the quality and the truthfulness with which they represent and promote the interests of the people."[131]

To say that every government depends on consent of the people does not, of course, mean that the subjects of all rulers *prefer* the established order to any other which might be created. They *may* consent because they positively approve of it—but they may also consent because they are unwilling to pay the price for the refusal of consent.[132] Refusal requires self-confidence and the motivation to resist and may involve considerable inconvenience[133] and social disruption,[134] to say nothing of suffering.

The degree of liberty or tyranny in any government is, it follows, in large degree a reflection of the relative determination of the subjects to be free and their willingness and ability to resist efforts to enslave them.

Three of the most important factors in determining to what degree a ruler's power will be controlled or uncontrolled therefore are: 1) the relative desire of the populace to control his power; 2) the relative strength of the subjects' independent organizations and institutions; and 3) the subjects' relative ability to withhold their consent and assistance.

Ultimately, therefore, freedom is not something which a ruler "gives" his subjects. Nor, in the long run, do the formal institutional structures and procedures of the government, as prescribed by the constitution, by themselves determine the degree of freedom or the limits of the ruler's power. A society may in fact be more free than those formal arrangements would indicate. Instead, the extent and intensity of the ruler's power will be set by the strength of the subjects and the condition of the whole society. Those limits may themselves, in turn, be expanded or contracted by the interplay between the actions of the ruler and those of the subjects.

The political conclusions to be drawn from these insights into the power of all rulers are simple but they are of fundamental significance in establishing control over dictators and finding a substitute for war. Errol E. Harris has formulated them succinctly. He argues that political power "can never be exercised without the acquiescence of the people—without the direct cooperation of the large numbers of people and the indirect cooperation of the entire community."[135] Therefore, tyranny has "flourished only where the people through ignorance, or disorganization, or by actual connivance and complicity, aid and abet the tyrant and keep him in power by allowing themselves to be the instruments of his coercion."[136]

> . . . a nation gets the government which it deserves, and those to whom this dictum is distasteful are either the small minority of dissidents, too few to influence the popular will of which they are the victims, or else those whose discontent is inconsistent with their practice, and who cooperate with the tyranny they deplore in spite of themselves and often without realizing it.[137]

Leo Tolstoy had such insights into the nature of all government in mind when he wrote about the English subjection of India:

> A commercial company enslaved a nation comprising two hundred millions. Tell this to a man free from superstitution and he will fail to grasp what these words mean. What does it mean that thirty thousand men . . . have subdued two hundred million . . . ? Do not the figures make it clear that it is not the English who have enslaved the Indians, but the Indians who have enslaved themselves?[138]

It was not simply English military might which subjected India to English rule, argued Tolstoy; this subjection could not be understood except in the context of the condition of Indian society which led the Indians to cooperate with, submit to, and obey the new *Raj*.

Such obedience and cooperation are not offered automatically, for people do not give equal obedience and help to every person and group which lays claim to governing them. Nor does any particular ruler necessarily receive equal obedience and assistance throughout his reign.

## B. Consent can be withdrawn

We have seen that obedience by the subject is the consequence of the mutual influence of various causes operating through his will. These causes of obedience are not, however, constant. The reasons for obedience are variable and may be strengthened or weakened. For example, the degree of a ruler's authority will vary. Other reasons for obedience may increase or decrease. Conditions and outlooks, the state of the subjects' knowledge, their attitudes and emotions—all may change. They may alter the subjects' willingness to submit or to resist. Even fear of sanctions is not constant. Such fear may grow because of increased severity or personal insecurity. Or it may decrease, because of reduced severity or increased willingness to accept sanctions because of overriding goals. The subjects' willingness to submit to a particular policy or to a whole regime may also be altered because of new beliefs (or new insights into old ones) and because of changes in perceptions of the established system. As a result of all these possible variations, the necessary consent of the subjects is unstable. It is always characterized by minor variations; it may at times be characterized by major changes.

Obedience therefore varies. For example, decline in the ruler's authority may undermine the subjects' willingness to obey and also weaken their voluntary cooperation.[139] When one or more reasons for obedience lose strength, the ruler may seek to counteract that loss by efforts to increase other reasons for obedience, such as by making sanctions harsher and more frequent or by increasing rewards for loyal service.[140] If such efforts are not successful, the continued decline in grounds for obedience may lead to the disintegration of the particular regime.

The change in the subjects' wills may lead to their withdrawing from the ruler their service, cooperation, submission and obedience. This withdrawal may occur among both the ordinary subjects and the ruler's agents and administrators. There is abundant historical evidence that changes in the opinions of the subjects and agents have led to reduced obedience and cooperation with the established ruler and, in turn, to the weakening of the regime.

The attitudes and beliefs of the ruler's agents are especially important here. Destroy the opinion of the supporting intermediary class that it is in their interest to support the ruler, urged Godwin, "and the fabric which is built upon it falls to the ground."[141] Likewise, he argued, any army, domestic or foreign, which is used to hold a people in subjection may be influenced by the opinions and sentiments of the people at large. The army may then decline to provide the ruler with assistance in suppressing the people, just as the general populace may withhold its assistance.[142]

Gandhi, who experimented widely with the political potentialities of disobedience, emphasized the importance of a change of will as as a prerequisite for a change in patterns of obedience and cooperation. There was, he argued, a need for: 1) a psychological change away from passive submission to self-respect and courage;[143] 2) recognition by the subject that his assistance makes the regime possible;[144] and 3) the building of a determination to withdraw cooperation and obedience.[145] Gandhi felt that these changes could be consciously influenced, and he therefore deliberately set out to bring them about. "My speeches," he said, "are intended to create 'disaffection' as such, that people might consider it a shame to assist or cooperate with a government that had forfeited all title to respect or support.''[146]

Changes in the attitudes of workers in factories or of citizens in politics, for example, which result in withdrawal of obedience and cooperation can create extreme difficulties for the system. It can be disrupted or paralyzed. At times this can happen even when the ruler's own agents continue their loyal obedience. The sheer difficulties of maintaining the normal working of any political unit when its subjects are bent upon an attitude of defiance and acts of obstruction are sufficient to give any ruler cause for thought. Without the obedience, cooperation, assistance and submission of the subjects and agents, power-hungry men claiming to be rulers would be "rulers" without subjects, and therefore only "objects of derision.''[147]

If a ruler's power is to be controlled by withdrawing help and obedience, noncooperation and disobedience must be widespread and must be maintained in the face of repression aimed at forcing a resumption of submission. However, once there has been a major reduction of or an end to the subjects' fear, and once there is a willingness to suffer sanctions as the price of change, large-scale disobedience and noncooperation become possible. Such action then becomes politically significant,[148] and the ruler's will is thwarted in proportion to the number of disobedient subjects and the degree of his dependence upon them. The answer to the problem of uncontrolled power may therefore lie in learning how to carry out and maintain such withdrawal despite repression.

# TOWARD A THEORY OF NONVIOLENT CONTROL OF POLITICAL POWER

Many people may readily admit that noncooperation and disobedience may create minor and temporary problems for rulers, but deny that such action can do more. If such were the limits of the impact of noncooperation and disobedience, then reliance would have to be placed elsewhere for control of the power of governments. Indeed, a number of political theorists have pointed to very different means of control over ruler's powers, and their theories have gained wide acceptance.

## A. Traditional controls

Because a discussion of these more traditional means of control can, by comparison and contrast, help to point up important characteristics of the nonviolent approach, they should be briefly surveyed here. Generally speaking, they fall into three categories: voluntary self-restraint by rulers themselves, institutional arrangements designed to limit the exercise of power, and the application of superior power of the same type, as in violent revolution or war.

**1. Self-restraint**    Self-restraint has long been one of the important restraining or limiting influences on rulers: the ruler voluntarily accepts some limits on the scope of his power and on the means he would use to wield that power. Beyond such limits he would be unwilling to go, because of a belief that to do so would violate moral and other standards accepted by the ruler and by society. This self-restraint has operated both alone and in combination with other controls, especially certain institutional arrangements which are discussed below.

Among contemporary writers, Martin J. Hillenbrand has placed special emphasis on the importance of self-control in rulers, regarding it as one of the two fundamental ways of controlling "the power of force" (the other being "the superior power of force").[149] He calls this "the internal control of self-restraint in the use of power based on some criterion or theory of conduct."[150] Hillenbrand concludes that for the present and in the future "the essential solution" to the problem of the control of power "must lie in the inducement of restraint in the·possessors of power so that they will use it only in accordance with certain criteria."[151]

**2. Institutional arrangements**    The second traditional means to control the abuse of power has been the attempt to establish "a principle or a set of institutions by which governments might be restrained."[152] This has involved setting up procedures for selecting the power-holder, determining government policy, and regulating government actions. The institutional and constitutional arrangements of liberal democracies have been the prime contributions toward this type of control. The legislature is elected by the subjects, and then either the executive is chosen by the legislature (as a prime minister and his cabinet) or the chief executive is elected directly by the subjects (as the American president). Governmental powers and procedures have been enumerated in the constitution, laws and traditions of such systems. In the American system differing tasks have been assigned to separate branches of the government, and the rights of the subjects have been enumerated. The judiciary has often been authorized to defend the rights of the subjects and to limit the actions of the government. These are only examples. Such systems are based on the assumption that in the last analysis the elected government is willing to abide by such restrictions on its power, and that powerful internal forces do not handicap seriously or disrupt the normal functioning of the system.

**3. Applying superior means of violence**     Where all other means of asserting influence and control over a  political ruler have failed, the traditional solution has been to threaten or to use superior violence against his forces. As we noted, Hillenbrand speaks of "the threat of, or the actual use of, superior power of force" as one of "two fundamental ways by which the power of force may be controlled."[153] Violence for this purpose has taken a variety of forms, including rioting, assassination, violent revolution, guerrilla warfare, *coup d'état,* civil war and international war.

The need for some further means of control beyond these three has often been admitted. Jouvenel, for example, has spoken of the difficulty of finding "some practical method" for controlling power,[154] and Jacques Maritain has posed "the problem of the means through which the people can supervise or control the State."[155]

This is not an easy task, for an alternative technique of control over political power ought to contain the potential for dealing with extreme situations as well as minor ones. The remainder of this chapter, therefore, surveys briefly a small part of the evidence from existing theory and practice which indicates that withdrawal of cooperation, obedience and submission may threaten the ruler's position and power.

## B. Theorists on withdrawal of support

Several political theorists have also argued that the withdrawal of obedience, cooperation and submission by subjects, if sustained, will produce a crisis for the ruler, threatening the very existence of the regime. These include Boétie, Machiavelli and Austin. The similarities of their views to the conclusion reached to this point in our analysis are striking.

Boétie—the least known of these theorists—argued that refusal of assistance to tyrants cuts off the sources of their power, and continued refusal causes tyrants to collapse without need for violence against them. ". . . if they are given nothing, if they are not obeyed, without fighting, without striking a blow, they remain naked and undone, and do nothing further, just as the root, having no soil or food, the branch withers and dies."[156] Boétie maintained that people could deliver themselves from a tyrant by casting off servility: ". . . just don't support him, and you will see him like a great colossus whose base has been stolen, of his own weight sink to the ground and shatter."[157] Boétie's views—reputedly written at the age of eighteen—exerted a great influence upon Thoreau and Tolstoy.[158] Through Tolstoy, those views also influenced Gandhi who saw in them a confirmation of the theory of power he had already grasped, and the political potential which he had already begun to explore.

A few years before Boétie, Machiavelli also pointed to the dangers which disobedience (by both his agents and his ordinary subjects) presented to a prince, especially in times of transition from a civil to an absolute order of government. The prince must then depend on the uncertain goodwill of his agents (magistrates), who may refuse to assist him, or of his subjects, who may not be "of a mind to obey him amid these confusions."[159] Machiavelli argued that the prince ". . . who has the public as a whole for his enemy can never make himself secure; and the greater his cruelty, the weaker does his regime become."[160]

Marat, writing in the *Ami du Peuple* on June 30, 1790, warned the "aristocracy of rich men" that, instead of taking revenge, the poor should simply leave the rich to themselves, for ". . . to take your place, we have only to stand with folded arms. Reduced, as you will then be, to working with your hands and tilling your own fields, you will become our equals . . ."[161]

Percy B. Shelley, poet and son-in-law of Godwin, was similarly convinced that by noncooperation numerically overwhelming subjects might control their rulers. His wife, Mary Wollstonecraft Shelley, has written: "The great truth that the many, if accordant and resolute, could control the few . . . made him long to teach his injured countrymen how to resist."[162]

Jouvenel, one of today's major political philosophers, has emphasized the dependence of earlier rulers on their subjects. How could a feudal king have waged "war if the barons had not mustered their contingents? What use to condemn a notable if his peers were certain to refuse to cooperate in the execution of the sentence?"[163] Not only the nobility but also the common people possessed power over the ruler through noncooperation: ". . . how could a feudal king have mustered an army if the barons . . . had not received obedience in their domains? And how could the industrialists have paid their taxes if their workers had stopped work?"[164]

It is almost axiomatic that in the face of such noncooperation and disobedience from anything less than the total population, the ruler will inflict severe sanctions through those agents remaining faithful to him. Repression of the subjects in such situations may force a resumption of submission. But repression will not necessarily ward off the danger to his position and power. As we have seen, disobedient subjects may still refuse to submit and may be willing to endure the repression and to continue their resistance in order to achieve some overriding objective. The subjects may then win, for, as Tocqueville argued, "A government which should have no other means of exacting obedience than open war must be very near its ruin . . ."[165]

Austin was similarly convinced:

For if the bulk of the community were fully determined to destroy it [the government], and to brave and endure the evils through which they must pass to their object, the might of the government itself, with the might of the minority attached to it, would scarcely suffice to preserve it, or even to retard its subversion. And though it were aided by foreign governments, and therefore were more than a match for the disaffected and rebellious people, it hardly could reduce them to subjection, or constrain them to permanent obedience, in case they hated it mortally, and were prepared to resist it to the death.[166]

"It is easier to conquer than to rule," observed Rousseau.[167]

## C. Clues to the political impact of noncooperation

There is considerable historical evidence that the theoretical insights of Boétie, Machiavelli, Austin, Jouvenel and others are valid and that, at least in certain circumstances, noncooperation can be effective in controlling governments and other bodies that wield political power. Let us explore a few examples which show in diverse situations the dependence of the titular ruler on his bureaucracy and then on the mass of the general populace.

**1. Bureaucratic obstruction**     Three cases are offered to show the dependence of power-holders on their bureaucracy. The first of these involves the withholding of cooperation in a political situation with a high degree of support for the ruler (the American presidency). The second is an intermediary case, with civil servants acting in an atmosphere of reservation and hostility (Russia in 1921–22). In the third there is a high degree of outright resistance (the German bureaucracy against the Kapp *Putsch*).

*The United States.*     Richard Neustadt has documented the actual limitations on the power of the American president, especially those imposed by his own aides, bureaucracy and Cabinet. After analyzing several important cases in the administrations of Presidents Truman and Eisenhower, Neustadt concludes: *"The same conditions that promote his leadership in form preclude a guarantee of leadership in fact."*[168] The president has a "power problem":

This is the classic problem of the man on top of any political

# POWER

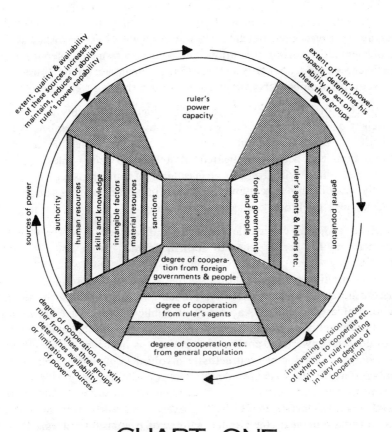

Chart labels (clockwise from top):

- ruler's power capacity
- extent of ruler's power capacity determines his ability to act on these three groups
- general population
- ruler's agents & helpers etc.
- foreign governments and people
- intervening decision process of whether to cooperate etc. with the ruler, resulting in varying degrees of cooperation
- degree of cooperation etc. from general population
- degree of cooperation from ruler's agents
- degree of cooperation from foreign governments & people
- degree of cooperation etc. with ruler from these three groups determines availability or limitation of sources of power
- sources of power
- authority
- human resources
- skills and knowledge
- intangible factors
- material resources
- sanctions
- extent, quality & availability of these sources increases, maintains, reduces or abolishes ruler's power capability

# CHART ONE
THIS IS A CONTINUAL PROCESS WHICH INCREASES OR DECREASES THE RULER'S POWER CAPACITY. THIS PROCESS ENDS ONLY WHEN THAT POWER IS DISINTEGRATED.

system: how to be on top in fact as well as name. It is a problem common to Prime Ministers and Premiers, and to dictators, however styled, and to kings who rule as well as reign. It is a problem also for the heads of private "governments," for corporate presidents, trade union leaders, churchmen.[169]

True, the position of the president gives him important persuasive and bargaining advantages, but these do not guarantee that his wishes will be implemented; all sorts of limitations and counterpressures confront him.[170] These come even from his executive officials, including White House aides and Cabinet members. Neustadt quotes a former Roosevelt aide:

> Half of a President's suggestions, which theoretically carry the weight of orders, can be safely forgotten by a Cabinet member. And if the President asks about a suggestion a second time, he can be told that it is being investigated. If he asks a third time, a wise Cabinet officer will give him at least part of what he suggests. But only occasionally, except about the most important matters, do Presidents ever get around to asking three times.

Neustadt adds that "this rule applies to staff as well as to the Cabinet, and certainly has been applied by staff in Truman's time and Eisenhower's."[171]

The limiting pressures on the effective power of the president extend, of course, far beyond the executive branch and include the attitudes and actions of private citizens, a variety of publics, and a vast network of institutions, political organizations, officials, personalities, and even foreign governments. Real government power "is influence of an effective sort on the behavior of men actually involved in making public policy and carrying it out"; the president's "power is the product of his vantage points in government, together with his reputation in the Washington community and his prestige outside."[172] Even clear commands are not always carried out, and command is a form of persuasion not suitable for everyday use.[173] While in office President Truman once said: "I sit here all day trying to persuade people to do things they ought to have sense enough to do without my persuading them. . . . That's all the powers of the President amount to." This limitation, Neustadt writes, points to "the essence of the problem," for " 'powers' are no guarantee of power . . ."[174]

In the summer of 1952, before the heat of campaign, President Truman contemplated the problems of a general-become-president should Eisenhower win the election: "He'll sit here," (tapping his desk for emphasis), "and he'll say, 'Do this! Do that!' *And nothing will happen.* Poor Ike—it won't be a bit like the Army. He'll find it very frustrating."[175]

Even as late as 1958 President Eisenhower still experienced " 'shocked surprise' that orders did not carry themselves out" and that the assistance of others had to be deliberately cultivated in order to produce "effective power."[176] Of course, it is possible to cultivate the art of inducing others to provide necessary help. However, the necessity to do this helps to confirm the pluralistic-dependency theory of power, the need of a power-holder to receive his power from others.

*The Soviet Union.* In March 1922, at the Eleventh Congress of the Russian Communist Party, Lenin presented the Political Report of its Central Committee. In very clear terms Lenin stated that "the political lesson" of 1921 had been that control of the seats of power does not necessarily mean control of the bureaucracy. Asking what constituted Communist strength and what the Party lacked, Lenin observed that "We have quite enough political power . . . The main economic power is in our hands." Nevertheless, something was missing. This, it was "clear," was lack of culture among the stratum of Communists who perform the functions of administration." In Moscow there were 4,700 responsible Communists and also the Russian government's "huge bureaucratic machine, that huge pile." But, Lenin said, "we must ask: Who is directing whom?" Were the Communists directing? No, said Lenin. "To tell the truth, they are not directing, they are being directed." Remarkably, Lenin compared this domestic power problem to the international power problem of occupation of a defeated country by a foreign conqueror—something they had learned in their history lessons as children, said Lenin. The nation that conquers appears to be the conqueror and the nation that is vanquished appears to be the conquered nation. However, what really happens then depends, said Lenin, on the relative cultural level of the two nations. Despite the military realities, if the vanquished nation is more "cultural" than the conquering nation "the former imposes its . . . culture upon the conqueror."

Lenin then asked: "Has something like this happened in the capital of the R.S.F.S.R? Have the 4,700 Communists (nearly a whole army division, and all of them the very best) become influenced by an alien culture?" The "culture" of the "vanquished," though "at a miserably low and insignificant level," was, nevertheless, higher than that of the "responsible Communist adminstrators, for the latter lack administration ability."

Communists who are put at the head of departments—and sometimes artful saboteurs deliberately put them in these positions in order to use them as a shield—are often fooled. This is a very unpleasant admission . . . but . . . this is the pivot of the question. I think that this is the political lesson of the past year; and it is around this that the struggle will rage in 1922.

Will the responsible Communists of the R.S.F.S.R. and of the Russian Communist Party realize that they cannot administer; that they only imagine that they are directing, but actually, they are being directed? If they realize this they will learn, of course; for this business can be learnt. But one must study hard to learn it and this our people are not doing. They scatter orders right and left, but the result is quite different from what they want.[177]

*Germany.* The monarchist–military Kapp *Putsch* of 1920 against the new German Weimar Republic was defeated. According to the eminent German historian Erich Eyck, victory for the republic against this attempted *coup d'état* was won principally by "the general strike of the workers and the refusal of the higher civil servants to collaborate with their rebel masters."[178] Particular attention will be given here to the refusal of assistance by these civil servants and certain other key groups. A further description is offered in Chapter Two.

At the onset of the *Putsch*, the legal Ebert government had proclaimed that German citizens remained under obligation to be loyal to and obey it alone.[179] The resulting resistance of the civil servants took a variety of forms. The officers of the *Reichsbank* refused Kapp's request for ten million Marks because it lacked an authorized official signature—all the undersecretaries in the ministries had refused to sign. The bank's cashier rejected Kapp's own signature as worthless,[180] even though his troops occupied the capital and the legal government had fled.

Unable to obtain the cooperation of qualified men to form the promised cabinet of experts, the Kappists asked public patience with a government of inexperienced men.[181] Some cabinet posts were never filled.[182] Many officials already in government bureaus refused to assist the Kapp regime; those in the government grain bureau, for example, threatened to strike unless Kapp retired.[183]

Even lesser civil servants were not very helpful to those who had seized the pinnacle of power; as a result, hopelessly incompetent men were appointed to lesser but nonetheless important posts, such as directorship of the press bureau;[184] this weakened the Kapp regime. Even the noncooperation of clerks and typists was felt. When Kapp's daughter, who was to draft the new regime's manifesto to the nation, arrived at the Reich Chancellery on Saturday, March 13, she found no one to type for her—no one had turned up for work that day—and no typewriter; as a result, Kapp's manifesto was too late for the Sunday papers.[185] Many offices of the Defense Ministry were also vacant that day.[186] Toward the end even the Security Police turned against Kapp, demanding his resignation.[187]

Combined with a powerful general strike, the impact of such noncooperation was considerable. A specialist in the history of the *coup d'état* and a historian of the Kapp *Putsch*, Lieutenant Colonel D.J. Goodspeed, writes: "No government can function long without a certain necessary minimum of popular support and cooperation."[188]

**2. Popular noncooperation**     The need for popular cooperation and the danger to the regime when it is absent are suggested by two cases: the Indians under the British in 1930 and the Soviet peoples under the Germans, 1941-45. In both cases we shall cite the views of the occupation officials.

*India.* Jawaharlal Nehru's experience with noncooperation in the Indian struggle for independence led him to conclude: "Nothing is more irritating and, in the final analysis, harmful to a government than to have to deal with people who will not bend to its will, whatever the consequences."[189] Gandhi wrote: "If we are strong, the British become powerless."[190]

The British government seems to have agreed with Nehru and Gandhi. British officials saw large-scale noncooperation and civil disobedience as a threat and recognized the great potential of nonviolent struggle for the control of political power. Addressing both Houses of the Indian Legislative Assembly on July 9, 1930, during the noncooperation and civil disobedience movement of 1930-31 for independence (the *Swaraj satyagraha),* the British Viceroy, Lord Irwin (who was later to become Lord Halifax), rejected the view that this was "a perfectly legitimate form of political agitation."

In my judgment and that of my Government it is a deliberate attempt to coerce established authority by mass action, and for this reason, as also because of its natural and inevitable developments, it must be regarded as unconstitutional and dangerously subversive. Mass action, even if it is intended by its promoters to be nonviolent, is nothing but the application of force under another form, and, when it has as its avowed objective the making of Government impossible, a Government is bound either to resist or abdicate. The present Movement is exactly analogous to a general strike in an industrial country, which has for its purpose the coercion of Government by mass pressure as opposed to argument, and which a British Government recently found it necessary to mobilize all its resources to resist.

But in India the noncooperators had gone further; the All-India Working Committee of the Indian National Congress had "insidiously" attempted to undermine the allegiance of the government's police and troops. As a result, the Viceroy continued, the government had "no option" but to proclaim that body illegal. India needed to be protected from "principles so fundamentally destructive . . ."

Therefore it is that I have felt bound to combat these doctrines and to arm Government with such powers as seem requisite to deal with the situation. I fully realize that in normal times such special powers would be indefensible. But the times are not normal, and, if the only alternative is acquiescence in the result of efforts openly directed against the constituted Government of the King-Emperor, I cannot for one moment doubt on which side my duty lies . . . So long as the Civil Disobedience Movement persists, we must fight it with all our strength.[191]

It is remarkable to find the British Viceroy in essential agreement with Nehru, Gandhi and Tolstoy on the nature of British power in India and on the effective means of destroying the foreign *Raj.*

*The Soviet Union.* Conditions and events during the German occupation of major sections of the Soviet Union during World War II differed vastly from those prevailing in India during the British occupation. However, German experiences also led certain officials of Nazi agencies and officers of the army to the view that the cooperation and obedience of the population of these territories were needed in order to maintain the occupation regime.

In accordance with their racial ideology and policies (especially that of replacing the existing population with Germans), for a long time the Nazis did not even seek cooperation from the Eastern *Untermenschen* (subhumans). This case therefore represents an absence of cooperation by the population of the occupied areas rather than a deliberate refusal of cooperation when sought. The situation is not always clear, for many factors influenced the course of the occupation. The role of the absence of cooperation in the occupied territories is itself sometimes difficult to isolate, because of the war and guerrilla activities in these territories. Nevertheless, despite ideology, Nazi policies and war, some German officials and officers very significantly concluded that the subjects' cooperation was needed.

In his study of the occupation Alexander Dallin is able to cite many instances of Nazi officials and army officers who came to realize the need for such cooperation. For example, Kube, the *Reichskommissar* in Belorussia, slowly and reluctantly concluded that at least the passive support of the population was needed. In 1942 he became convinced, Dallin reports, "that German forces could not exercise effective control without enlisting the population." [192] Dallin also quotes a statement by German military commanders in the Soviet Union in December 1942: "The seriousness of the situation clearly makes imperative the positive cooperation of the population. Russia can be beaten only by Russians." [193] Captain Wilfried Strik-Strikfeldt expressed similar views in lectures before a General Staff training course: "Germany, Strik-Strikfeldt concluded, faced the choice of proceeding with or without the people: it could not succeed without them if only because such a course required a measure of force which it was incapable of marshalling." General Harteneck wrote in May 1943: "We can master the wide Russian expanse which we have conquered only with the Russians and Ukrainians who live in it, never against their will." [195]

Reviewing the history of the German occupation of the Soviet Union, Dallin writes:

> While the whip continued to be the rather universal attribute of German rule, there slowly matured an elementary realization that the active cooperation of the people was needed for maximum security and optimal performance. A pragmatic imperative, perceived primarily in the field, dictated a departure from the practice, if not the theory, of Nazi-style colonialism. [196]

This departure is all the more significant because it was diametrically opposed to the Nazi ideological position, which called the East Europeans subhumans, and to the earlier plans for exterminating the original population of major areas in order to provide empty territory for colonization, *Lebensraum* for the German *Volk*.

## D. Toward a technique of control of political power

In May 1943 Hitler told Alfred Rosenberg that in the occupied East, German policy needed to be so tough as to numb the population's political consciousness. [197] However, in July he also declared that:

> . . . ruling the people in the conquered regions is, I might say, of course a psychological problem. One cannot rule by force alone. True, force is decisive, but it is equally important to have this psychological something which the animal trainer also needs to be master of his beast. They must be convinced that we are the victors. [198]

What follows from Hitler's admission that "force" alone is inadequate in ruling people in conquered territories if the people refuse to accept the militarily successful invaders as their political masters? Hitler's emphasis on the psychological nature of occupation rule very significantly coincides with the views of the political thinkers which have already been presented: that in order to rule it is necessary to reach the subjects' minds. These theoretical insights into power indeed have practical implications. Noncooperation and defiance by subjects, at least under certain conditions, can create serious problems for rulers, thwart their intentions and policies, and even destroy their government.

If this is true, then *why* have people not long since abolished oppression, tyranny and exploitation? There appear to be several reasons. First, such victims of a ruler's power usually feel helpless in the face of his capacity for repression, punishment and control. These feelings of helplessness arise from several causes.

The subjects usually do not realize that they are the source of the ruler's power and that by joint action they could dissolve that power. Failure to realize the role they play may have its roots either in innocent ignorance or in deliberate deception by the ruler. If the subjects look at their ruler's power at a given moment, they are likely to see it as a hard, solid force which at any point may fall upon them in their helplessness; this short-range view leads them to the monolith theory of power. If they were to look at their ruler's power both backward and forward in time, however, and note its origins and growth, its variations and fragility, they would begin to see their role in the genesis, continuance and development of that power. This realization would reveal that they possess the capacity to destroy that power.

It is also often in the ruler's power-interest to keep the people deceived about the fragile nature of political power and their capacity to dissolve it. Hence, rulers may sometimes seek to keep this knowledge from them. Tolstoy argued that the people, on whose cooperation the oppressive regime ultimately depended, continued to serve it by becoming soldiers and police, because "from long continued deception they no longer see the connection between their bondage and their own share in the deeds of violence." [199] In his day Hume similarly anticipated that rulers would themselves see the dangers of this view of power to their own position:

> Were you to preach, in most parts of the world, that political connections are founded together on voluntary consent or a mutual promise, the magistrate would soon imprison you, as seditious, for loosening the

ties of obedience, if your friends did not before shut you up as delirious, for advancing such absurdities.[200]

Hobbes saw something of the power of disobedience and, anticipating that it would destroy *all* government (not only a particular one), he turned away horrified, arguing firmly for the universal (or near universal) unquestioning submission of subjects to rulers.[201]

Unjust or oppressive rulers have every reason to keep knowledge of this theory from their subjects, and there are signs that they deliberately do so. (It is much less obvious that governments which genuinely reflect the will of their subjects have good reason for such restriction.) Even small-scale strikes and trade unions were widely illegal until union organization became too strong to suppress. The frequent reactions of governments when confronted with general strikes and mass popular action are worth noting. Do they not react with disproportionately intense determination not to give in, to defeat such actions—*even when these actions have majority support* and are aimed at relatively minor objectives? Do not such governments often refuse to negotiate until the general strike has been called off? Even when concessions are made, are these not often attributed to causes other than the popular noncooperation? It would seem that at least part of the explanation for such reactions is that the governments often object less to granting the demands than they do to the popular withdrawal of cooperation and obedience, and that they fear the spread of an awareness of the power of noncooperation in controlling political power. This would also explain, among other things, why rulers who pride themselves on their liberalism and who acknowledge the right of individual dissent, even in conscientious objection to military service, may react so strongly when a number of individuals act collectively in noncooperation and disobedience.

We are assuming that, under at least certain circumstances, ethical justification for disobedience of commands of rulers, and even for the abolition of whole regimes, exists. This is an assumption which not everyone will grant, but it is not a question which any longer requires much debate. Always to deny such a right of disobedience or revolution is to say that once Hitler's Nazi regime came to power, it was the duty of all Germans to obey it completely and carry out all its plans efficiently, that no matter what it did, there was no right of resistance or revolution. Few today will accept so extreme an interpretation of one's duty to obey. If they do not accept it, they implicitly grant that disobedience and defiance may be morally justified, at least under certain conditions.

The right to disobey and resist has been argued, however, on other grounds as well. Hume, for example, believed that constitutional government, with its separation and limitation of powers, depended on some form of resistance to keep it democratic, for "every part or member of the constitution must have a right of self-defence, and of maintaining its ancient bounds against the encroachments of every other authority." It is, he argued,

> a gross absurdity to suppose in any government a right without a remedy, or allow that the supreme power is shared with the people, without allowing that it is lawful for them to defend their share against every invader. Those, therefore, who would seem to respect our free government, and yet deny the right of resistance, have renounced all pretensions to common sense, and do not merit a serious answer.[202]

The problem of finding remedies which are not in the long run worse than the evils they are intended to remove—a problem which concerned Hobbes—is still a difficult one. It is important to examine all proposed courses of action in that light, including the technique on which this book is focused. Examination of specific political potentialities of this technique lies outside the scope of this study, which is limited to exploration of the nature of nonviolent action; but an understanding of nonviolent action and its theory of power requires that this point be briefly answered. There is no reason to assume, as Hobbes did, that the withdrawal of obedience and cooperation to deal with a tyrant, for example, necessarily destroys all future capacity to maintain social order and democratic government. There are important reasons for believing that this is not true; these will become clearer as we consider in the concluding chapters the actual operation of the technique of action based upon this theory of power. There is even evidence that the alternative forms of behavior—violent counteraction or passive submission to oppression—may be more destructive of society than nonviolent action, especially under modern conditions.

Long before he became Chancellor, Hitler wrote that "one must not imagine that one could suddenly take out of a briefcase the drafts of a new State constitution" based on the leader-principle and impose them dictatorially on the State by command, "by a degree of power from above. One can try such a thing, but the result will certainly not be able to live, will in most cases be a stillborn child."[203] What would happen if people realized this on a wide scale, knew that they could prevent the imposition on them of unwanted policies and regimes, and were skillfully able to refuse to assist, in open struggle? It has been suggested that such knowledge could lead to the abolition of tyranny and oppression. Gandhi, for example, though referring specifically to economic issues, certainly had in mind wider implications when he wrote:

> The rich cannot accumulate wealth without the cooperation of the poor in society. If this knowledge were to penetrate to and spread amongst the poor, they would become strong and would learn how to free themselves by means of nonviolence from the crushing inequalities which have brought them to the verge of starvation.[204]

Harris has observed that people do not realize that ". . . political power is their own power. . . . Consequently, they become its accomplices at the same time as they become its victims. . . . If sufficient people understood this and really knew what they were about and how to go about it, they could ensure that government would never be tyrannical."[205] It is not without significance, perhaps, that the first issue of the first illegal resistance newspaper in Nazi-occupied Norway included this sentence near the conclusion of its first policy article: "We are convinced that a system which builds on hate, injustice and oppression never can last."[206]

The central political implications of our analysis point to control of political power by, in Green's words, "withdrawal by the sovereign people of power from its legislative or executive representatives."[207] It is control of the ruler's power by withdrawal of consent. It is control, not by the infliction of superior violence from on top or outside, not by persuasion, nor by hopes of a change of heart in the ruler, but rather by the subjects' declining to supply the power-holder with the sources of his power, by cutting off his power at the roots. This is resistance by noncooperation and disobedience. If it can be applied practically and can succeed despite repression, this would seem to be the most efficient and certain means for controlling power.

If this theory of power is to be implemented, the question is *how*. Lack of knowledge of how to act has also been one reason why people have not, long since, abolished tyranny and oppression.

First, the citizens' rejection of the tyrannical government must be actively expressed in refusal to cooperate. This refusal may take many forms; few of these will be easy, each will require effort, many will be dangerous, and all will need courage and intelligence. And there must be group or mass action. As Gaetano Mosca pointed out, the ruling minority is unified and can act in concert, whereas the ruled majority is "unorganized"[208]—or, we may add, often lacks independent organization. The result is that the subjects are usually incapable of corporate opposition and can be dealt with one by one. Effective action based on this theory of power requires *corporate* resistance and defiance—which may or may not be preceded by opportunity for advance specific preparations.

But generalized obstinacy and collective stubbornness are not effective enough. General opposition must be translated into a strategy of action, and people need to know how to wage the struggle which will almost inevitably follow their initial act of defiance. This includes how to persist despite repression. They will need to understand the technique based on this insight into power, including the methods of that technique, its dynamics of change, requirements for success and principles of strategy and tactics. The implementation must be skillful. We need, therefore, to examine in detail how the technique of nonviolent action—which is built on this insight into power—operates in struggle.

Therefore, we first turn to the exploration of the basic characteristics of the nonviolent technique and a survey of its history. This will lead us, in Part Two, into the multitude of specific nonviolent "weapons," or methods, included in its armory. The chapters of the concluding Part will examine in detail the dynamics and mechanisms of nonviolent struggle, and the factors which in a particular conflict determine its failure or its success.

# NOTES

1. Martin J. Hillenbrand, **Power and Morals** (New York: Columbia University Press, 1949), p. 12.
2. Robert M. MacIver, **The Web of Government** (New York: Macmillan, 1947), p. 87.
3. *Ibid.,* p. 83.
4. A number of respected political and social theorists and prominent political activists have assumed this view of the nature of power, although there have been few systematic presentations of it. One reason for this lack appears to be that many of the theorists have presumed the view to be so obvious that detailed analysis was thought to be unnecessary.
   For a brief presentation of this view of power, see Errol E. Harris, "Political Power," *Ethics,* vol. XLVIII, no. 1 (Oct. 1957). pp. 1-10. Dr. Harris' article came to my attention sometime after the early drafts of this analysis were completed.

5. Auguste Comte pointed to the close relationship between the society and the political system and their mutual influence on each other, emphasizing the need to view political systems in the context of "the coexisting state of civilization." (Auguste Comte, **The Positive Philosophy of Auguste Comte**. Freely trans. and condensed by Harriet Martineau, with an Introduction by Frederic Harrison, 2 vols. [London: George Bell & Sons, 1896], vol. II, pp. 220-223.) He lamented that "the existing political philosophy supposes the absence of any such interconnection among the aspects of society . . ." *(Ibid.,* p. 225.)

T. H. Green maintained that political theorists have often erred in focusing their attention solely on a coercive State and isolated individuals, ignoring other forms of community and the important role of society in influencing the nature of political power. (Thomas Hill Green, **Lectures on the Principles of Political Obligation.** [London: Longmans, Green & Co., 1948 (orig. 1882)], pp. 121 ff.)

"The notion that force is the creator of government," argued MacIver, "is one of those part-truths that beget total errors." (MacIver, **The Web of Government,** p. 15.)

More recently Errol E. Harris has written: "Physical force itself is the instrument only, not the essence, of political power. Brawn, guns, and batons are but the tools employed. Power itself is not a physical phenomenon at all, it is always and only a social phenomenon . . ." (Harris, "Political Power," p. 3.)

6. The term "ruler" or "rulers" is used here as a kind of shorthand to describe the individuals or groups which occupy the highest positions of decision and command in a given government. At times this "ruler" may be, or come close to being, a single person – as is usually assumed to have been true in the case of Hitler and Stalin. In other cases the "ruler" may be a small elite or an oligarchy. Most of the time, however, a very large number of persons, with complex interrelationships, may collectively occupy the position of "ruler." In a case of pure direct democracy, the position of "ruler" as separated from the "ruled" would not exist. Intermediary forms and gradations also exist.

7. Etienne de La Boetie, *"Discours de la Servitude Volontaire,"* in **Oeuvres Completes d'Etienne de la Boetie** (Paris: J. Rouam & Cie.,1892), p. 12. See also *Boetie,* **Anti-Dictator:** The *Discours sur la servitude volontaire"*Of Etinne de La Boetie, trans. by Harry Kurz (New York: Columbia University Press, 1942), pp. 11-12. That translation differs slightly from the one in the text of this volume which was made by Madeline Chevalier Emerick.

8. Comte saw "every social power" as being "constituted by a corresponding assent . . . of various individual wills, resolved to concur in a common action, of which this power is the first organ, and then the regulator. Thus, authority is derived from concurrence, and not concurrence from authority . . . so that no great power can arise otherwise than from the strongly prevalent disposition of the society in which it exists . . ." The degree of disposition in the society toward a ruler, Comte believed, would determine the relative strength or weakness of the power-holder. (Comte, **The Positive Philosophy of Auguste Comte,** pp. 222-223.)

9. Two contemporary American writers argue similarly to Comte. Harold D. Lasswell writes: "Power is an interpersonal situation; those who hold power are empowered. They depend upon and continue only so long as there is a continuing stream of empowering responses . . . power is . . . a process that vanishes when the supporting responses cease.

"The power relationship is . . . giving-and-taking. It is a cue-giving and cue-taking in a continuing spiral of interaction." (Harold D. Lasswell, **Power and Personality** [New York: W. W. Norton & Co., 1948], p. 10.)

MacIver says it this way: ". . . social power is in the last resort derivative, not inherent in the groups or individuals who direct, control or coerce other groups or individuals. The power a man has is the power he *disposes;* it is not intrinsically his own. He cannot command unless another obeys. He cannot control unless the social organization invests him with the apparatus of control." (MacIver, **The Web of Government,** pp. 107-108.)

10. Jacques Maritain, **Man and the State** (Chicago Ill.: University of Chicago Press, 1954, and London: Hollis and Carter, 1954), U.S. ed., p. 126; British ed., pp. 114-115.

11. John Austin, **Lectures on Jurisprudence or the Philosophy of Positive Law** (Fifth ed., rev. and ed. by Robert Campbell; 2 vols; London: John Murray, 1911 [1861], vol. I, p. 89.

12. Charles Louis de Secondat, Baron de Montesquieu, **The Spirit of the Laws** (Trans. by Thomas Nugent; Introduction by Franz Neumann; New York: Haffner, 1949), vol. I, p. 313.

13. Arthur Livingstone emphasized the closeness of the relationship between possession of the sources of power and being a ruler: "A man rules or a group of men rules when the man or the group is able to control the social forces that, at the given moment in the given society, are essential to the possession and retention of power." Social forces are defined by Livingstone as "any human activity or perquisite that has a social significance – money, land, military prowess, religion, education, manual labor, science – anything." (Arthur Livingstone, Introduction to Gaetano Mosca, **The Ruling Class** (Trans. by Hannah D. Kahn; ed. and rev. with an Introduction by Arthur Livingstone; New York and London: McGraw-Hill, 1939), p. xix.

14. Rousseau speaks "of morality, of custom, above all of public opinion" as "the real constitution of the State" upon which "success in everything else depends." (Jean Jacques Rousseau, "The Social Contract," in **The Social Contract and Discourses** [New York: E. P. Dutton & Co., 1920, and London: J. M. Dent & Sons, Ltd., 1920], p. 48.)

15. While acknowledging the role of coercive force, David Hume points out that "nothing but their own consent, and their sense of the advantages resulting from peace and order" could be responsible for the subjection of multitudes to a ruler. (Frederick Watkins, ed., **Hume: Theory of Politics** [Edinburgh: Thomas Nelson & Sons, Ltd., 1951], p. 196.) It is, Hume says, "on opinion only that government is founded," including not only the most free and popular, but also the most despotic and military ones. *(Ibid.* p. 148.)
William Godwin argues that it is precisely *because* government is based upon opinion and consent that rulers use various pressures to influence the subjects to accept their authority. (William Godwin, **Enquiry Concerning Political Justice and its Influence on Morals and Happiness** [Sec. ed.; London: G. G. and J. Robinson, 1796], vol. I, p. 98.)

16. Bertrand de Jouvenel, **On Power: Its Nature and The History of its Growth** (Trans. by J. F. Huntington; Boston: Beacon Paperback, 1962), p. 355. British edition: **Power: The Natural History of its Growth** (Revised; London: The Batchworth Press, 1952), p. 302.

17. Green, **Lectures . . . ,** p. 103. Habitual obedience, he argued, arises from "the common will and reason of men," and only rarely needs backing by coercive force. (*Ibid.;* see also p. 98.) Coercive force, says Green, is not the most important thing about governments; it is not coercive power operating on the fears of the subjects "which determines their habitual obedience." *(Ibid.,* pp. 98 and 103.)

That would require far, far more police than there are; Jouvenel says as many police as subjects. (Jouvenel, **On Power,** p. 376. Br. ed.: **Power,** p. 317.) Even where people have been conquered by military might, the dominance cannot last if it depends solely upon such means (MacIver, **The Web of Government,** p. 16; Chester I. Barnard, **The Functions of the Executive** [Cambridge, Mass.: Harvard University Press, 1948], p. 149). Even the power of undemocratic regimes depends on acceptance of their authority. (Harris, "Political Power" p. 6.) Rousseau insisted: "The strongest is never strong enough to be always master, unless he transforms his strength into right, and obedience into duty." (Rousseau, "The Social Contract," p. 8.)

Niccolo Machiavelli speaks repeatedly in **The Prince** of the need to keep subjects satisfied and loyal, to maintain or win their good will, and of the importance of avoiding their hatred. (Machiavelli, **The Prince** [New York: E. P. Dutton & Co., Everyman's Library, 1948, and London: J. M. Dent & Sons, Everyman's Library, 1948], pp. 16, 74-77, 81-82, 129 and 146-147.) In his **Discourses** Machiavelli writes that the prince "who has the public as a whole for his enemy can never make himself secure; and the greater his cruelty, the weaker does his regime become. In such a case the best remedy he can adopt is to make the populace his friend." (Machiavelli, "The Discourses on the First Ten Books of Livy," **The Discourses of Niccolo Machiavelli** [London: Routledge and Kegan Paul, 1950]), vol. I, p. 254.

18. W. A. Rudlin, "Obedience, Political," **Encyclopedia of the Social Sciences,** (New York: Macmillan, 1935), vol. XI, p. 415.

19. Says Green: "If a despotic government comes into anything like habitual conflict with the unwritten law which represents the general will, its dissolution is beginning . . ." (Green, **Lectures . . . ,** p. 313.)

Jouvenel points out that in the extremity of the total rejection of the ruler's claimed authority, he would simply not have the attributes of a ruler. The State "falls to pieces as soon as the authority of the sovereign loses its hold on a part of the subject mass, which bestows its allegiance elsewhere." (Bertrand de Jouvenel, **Sovereignty: An Enquiry into the Political Good** [Chicago, Ill.: University of Chicago Press, 1959, and London: The Batchworth Press, 1952], p. 4.)

Without authority, says MacIver, organizations can "carry no function whatever." (MacIver, **The Web of Government,** p. 84.) "Even the most ruthless tyrant gets nowhere unless he can clothe himself with authority." *(Ibid.,* p. 83.) In a situation where a considerable portion of the subjects rejects the ruler's authority while another considerable portion continues to accept it, his political power will be seriously weakened, but not necessarily destroyed. Two States will then tend to form and will engage in some form of struggle which will lead to the destruction of one (as in a civil war), or to some kind of accommodation (ranging from reforms to separation into two independent States, e.g., in colonial conflicts).

20. Max Weber, "Politics as a Vocation," in **From Max Weber: Essays in Sociology** (Trans., ed. and with an Introduction by H. H. Gerth and C. Wright Mills; New York: Oxford University Press, Galaxy Book, 1958 [orig. 1946], and London: Kegan Paul, Trench, Trabner and Co., 1948), p. 81.

21. See Bernard, **The Functions of the Executive,** pp. 181-182.

22. *Ibid.,* p. 182.

23. Herbert Goldhamer and Edward A. Shils point out that full control is rarely possible over a large subordinate staff, and hence the subordinates may assume a certain amount of independence and initiative in wielding power. This,

combined with the ruler's dependence on them, ". . . tends to set up a bilateral power relation between the chief power-holder and his subordinates, giving the latter power over the chief power-holder in addition to any independent power they may exercise over the mass. Subordinate power-holders, to the extent that they exercise independent power in the sphere claimed by the chief power-holder, will limit the power of the latter, and to that extent lose their character of subordinates." (Herbert Goldhamer and Edward A. Shils, "Power and Status," in The American Journal of Sociology, vol. XLV, no. 2 [September 1939], p. 177.) A ruler, over a period of time, must therefore come to terms with his subjects and adjust to some degree to their needs and aspirations. (See Jouvenel, On Power, p. 110; Br. ed.: Power, p. 101.)

24. Barnard insists: ". . . no absolute or external authority can compel the necessary effort beyond a minimum insufficient to maintain efficient or effective organization performance." (Barnard, The Functions of the Executive, p. 182.) He argues that this need for contributions is a common characteristic of all institutions including the State. Most attempted organizations fail because "they . . . cannot secure sufficient contributions of personal efforts to be effective or cannot induce them on terms that are efficient." Such failure occurs, in the last analysis, because "the individuals in sufficient numbers . . . withdraw or withhold the indispensable contributions."(Ibid., pp. 164-165).

25. Jouvenel, Sovereignty, p. 4.

26. MacIver, The Web of Government, p. 16.

27. As Harris has pointed out: ". . . there is no such thing as political enforcement which is not a socially exercised activity in which a considerable proportion of the members of the group on which it is imposed participate." (Harris, "Political Power," p. 6.) Both the manufacture and the use of the instruments applied in inflicting violent political sanctions depend on "that very social organization which the political power is needed to maintain." (Ibid., p. 4; see also pp. 3-5).

28. Karl W. Deutsch, "Cracks in the Monolith," in Carl J. Friedrich, ed., Totalitarianism (Cambridge, Mass.: Harvard University Press, 1954), p. 315.

29. Rudlin, "Obedience, Political," p. 416.

30. Deutsch, "Cracks in the Monolith," pp. 314-315.

31. Deutsch writes: "At one end of this spectrum, we could imagine a situation where everybody obeys habitually all commands or decisions of the totalitarian regime, and no enforcement is necessary; at the other end . . . we could imagine a situation where nobody obeys voluntarily any decision of the totalitarian system, and everybody has to be compelled to obey at pistol point, or under conditions of literally ever-present threat and ever-present supervision.
"In the first of these cases, enforcement would be extremely cheap and, in fact, unnecessary; in the second, it would be prohibitively expensive, and in fact no government could be carried on on such a basis. Even the behavior of an occupying army in wartime in enemy territory falls far short of this standard; even there, many of its orders are obeyed more or less habitually by an unwilling population in situations where immediate supervision is not practicable. If the occupying army had to put a soldier behind every man, woman, and child of the local population, it would be extremely difficult for the army to keep sufficient numbers of its men detached from such occupation duties to continue with further military operations. Somewhere in the middle between these extremes of universal compliance and ubiquitous enforcement is the range of effective government. There a majority of individuals in a majority of

situations obeys the decisions of the government more or less from habit without any need for immediate supervision." *(Ibid.,* pp. 313-314.)

32. Livingstone, "Introduction," to Mosca, **The Ruling Class,** p. xix.

33. As Jeremy Bentham put it: "The efficacy of power is, in part at least, in proportion to the promptitude of obedience ..." (Jeremy Betham, **A Fragment on Government** [ Ed. with an Introduction by F. C. Montague; London: Oxford University Press, Humphrey Milford, 1931 (orig. 1891) ] ,p. 168. ) The degree of political power is established by "neither more nor less ... than a habit of, and disposition to obedience ..." *(Ibid.,* p. 223.)
    The need for obedience is not limited to free societies argued Montesquieu: In despotic states, the nature of government requires the most passive obedience ..." (Montesquieu,The **Spirit of the Laws,**vol. I, p. 2.)
    Weber said it concisely: "If the state is to exist, the dominated must obey the authority claimed by the powers that be." (Weber, "Politics as a Vocation," p. 78.)

34. Jouvenel, **On Power,** p. 18; Br. ed.: **Power,** pp. 27-28.

35. Kurt H. Wolff, editor and trans., **The Sociology of Georg Simmel** (Glencoe, Ill.: Free Press, 1950), p. 183.

36. **The Shorter Oxford English Dictionary on Historical Principles,** Third Edition, revised, 2 vols. (Oxford: The Clarendon Press, 1959), vol. II, pp. 2060 and 2084.

37. "Although cue-giving is highly concentrated in the conductor, commanding officer or foreman, the function is not wholly monopolized by any of them. The conductor, for instance, is continuously responsive to what comes to his attention from the orchestra; and neither the drill master nor the foreman is oblivious to the behavior of his men. And the members of the orchestra, the squad or the work-team are attentive to one another, adapting themselves to one another's performance." (Lasswell, **Power and Personality,** pp. 10-11.)

38. *Ibid.,* p. 12.

39. *Ibid.,* p. 16.

40. Wolff, ed., **The Sociology of Georg Simmel,** p. 183.

41. *Ibid.,* p. 186.

42. *Ibid.*

43. *Ibid.,* p. 250.

44. Barnard, **The Functions of the Executive,** pp. 181-182.

45. *Ibid.,* p. 182.

46. These same principles apply despite the fact that on relatively minor issues the supporting units of the State will usually support "law and order" regardless of the merits of the case, and despite the fact that the pressure on individual subjects to conform will be strong. *(Ibid.,* p. 183.)

47. E. V. Walter writes: "A power relation ... is a dynamic interaction in which at least some control may be exercised by all parties. It is clear, of course, that each does not control the others to the same degree, nor do they control the same thing." (E. V. Walter, "Power and Violence," **American Political Science Review,** vol. LVIII, no. 2, [June 1964], p. 352.)

48. Franz Neumann, **The Democratic and The Authoritarian State: Essays in Political and Legal Theory** (Ed. and with a Preface by Herbert Marcuse; Glencoe, Ill.: Free Press and Falcon's Wing Press, 1957), p. 3.

49. Paul Pigors offers a fourth variable: the presence or absence of a common cause uniting the ruler and subject. This factor is here included in the situation. See

Paul Pigors, **Leadership or Domination** (New York: Houghton Mifflin Co., 1935, and London: George G. Harrap, 1935), p. 195. See also Mary Follett, **Creative Experience** (New York and London: Longmans, Green & Co., 1924), p. 61.

50. Jouvenel, **On Power,** p. 17; Br. ed.: **Power,** p. 27. Jouvenel uses the term "Power" with a capital "P" as approximately the same as "the State."

51. "Discipline on such a scale as this," wrote Jacques Necker, "must astound any man who is capable of reflection. This obedience on the part of a very large number to a very small one is a thing singular to observe and mysterious to think on." (Necker, **Du Pouvoir Executif dans les Grandes Etats** [1792], pp. 20-22; quoted in Jouvenel, **On Power,** p. 19; Br. ed.: **Power,** pp. 28-29.)
It was Hume's question too: "Nothing appears more surprising, to those who consider human affairs with a philosophical eye, than the easiness with which the many are governed by the few, and the implicit submission with which men resign their own sentiments and passions to those of their rulers." (Watkins, ed., **Hume,** p. 148.)
Contemporary political thinkers are still asking the same question. Hans Gerth and C. Wright Mills have written: "Since power implies that an actor can carry out his will, power involves obedience. The general problem of politics accordingly is the explanation of varying distributions of power and obedience, and one basic problem of political psychology is why men in their obedience accept others as the powerful. Why do they obey?" (Hans Gerth and C. Wright Mills, **Character and Social Structure** [New York: Harcourt, Brace & Co., 1953, and London: Routledge and Kegan Paul, 1954], p. 193.)

52. In the sixteenth century Boetie marvelled at the phenomenon of obedience to oppressors: ". . . what happens in every country, by all men, and in all eras, that one man abuses a hundred thousand and deprives them of their liberty, who would believe it, if only he heard of it, and did not see it? And if it only happened in strange and distant lands and that it was spoken of, who would not suppose that it was somewhat false and made up, not really true?" (Boetie, "Discours de la Servitude Volontaire," p. 8; see also, Boetie, **Anti-Dictator,** p. 9.)

53. Gerth and Mills, **Character and Social Structure,** p. 194.

54. Thomas Hobbes, **Leviathan** (Reprinted from the edition of 1651; New York: E. P. Dutton, 1950 and Oxford: Clarendon Press, 1958), U.S. ed., p. 167; Br. ed., p. 152.

55. Jouvenel, **On Power,** p. 22; Br. ed.: **Power,** p. 30. See also Deutsch, "Cracks in the Monolith," p. 314; MacIver, **The Web of Government,** p. 76; Green, **Lectures . . . ,** pp. 101 and 126; Austin, **Lectures . . . ,** pp. 292-294; and Necker, quoted in Jouvenel, **On Power,** pp. 21-22; Br. ed.: **Power,** p. 30.

56. Watkins, ed., **Hume,** p. 155. See also p. 197.

57. Austin, **Lectures . . . ,** p. 294.

58. Jouvenel, **On Power,** pp. 23-24; Br. ed.: **Power,** p. 32.

59. See, e.g., Neumann, **The Democratic and the Authoritarian State,** p. 8; MacIver, **The Web of Government,** pp. 76-77; Jouvenel, **Sovereignty,** p. 2; Deutsch, "Cracks in the Monolith," p. 314; Rudlin, "Obedience, Political," p. 417; Austin, **Lectures . . . ,** p. 298; Watkins, ed., **Hume,** pp. 201-206; Godwin, **Enquiry . . . ,** vol. II, pp. 43-44; and Hobbes, **Leviathan,** U.S. ed., p. 167; Br. ed., p. 152.

60. Green, **Lectures . . . ,** p. 98.

61. Machiavelli, although emphasizing the need for the goodwill of the populace if a prince were to maintain his power, believed that under certain conditions

obedience could be produced by sufficient violence and threat of violence. (See, e.g., Machiavelli, **The Prince**, p. 67.) Leo Tolstoy, too, emphasized the role of fear of sanctions in obtaining obedience to the State, especially in cases where obedience was not in the interest of the subjects. (See, e.g., Leo Tolstoy, **The Kingdom of God Is Within You** [New York: Thomas Y. Crowell, 1899, and London: William Heinemann, 1894], U.S. ed., pp. 154-155, 263-264, 266; Br. ed., pp. 237, 413, 417.

62. See e.g., Watkins, ed., Hume, pp. 154-155; Mosca, **The Ruling Class**, pp. 53-54; and Bertrand Russell, **Power: A New Social Analysis** (New York: W. W. Norton & Co., 1938; and London: Geo. Allen and Unwin, 1938), U.S. ed., p. 184; Br. ed.: p. 190.

63. Montesquieu, for example, found it under both monarchies and republics, (See, Montesquieu, **The Spirit of the Laws**, vol. I, p. 34). Contemporary writers such as Jouvenel, have found it "varying in liveliness and effectiveness from one individual to another, among the members of any political society." (Jouvenel, **Sovereignty**, p. 87.)

64. See MacIver, **The Web of Government**, p. 77, and Green, **Lectures . . .** , pp. 123-124.

65. Feelings of moral obligation as a cause of obedience may be variously interpreted; ranging from Green's view that this is largely a recognition of the objective social benefits of government, to the anarchist view that this is always a means of deception used to hold the people in subjection. (See Godwin, **Enquiry . . .** , vol. I, p. 98, and Emma Goldman's pamphlet **The Individual, Society and the State** (Chicago: Free Society Forum, n.d.), p. 5.

66. Green, **Lectures . . .** , pp. 123-124.

67. See Barnard, **The Functions of the Executive**, pp. 152-153.

68. Jouvenel, **On Power**, p. 376; Br. ed.: **Power**, p. 317.

69. *Ibid.,* p. 302.

70. See Hume's two-fold classification of (1) "opinion of interest," including consideration (a) in this text, and (2)"opinion of right," including (b), (c), and (d). Watkins, ed., **Hume**, pp. 148-150.

71. Green, **Lectures . . .** , p. 125.

72. Watkins, ed., **Hume**, pp. 102 and 213.

73. *Ibid.,* p. 101.

74. Green, **Lectures . . .** , pp. 124-125. Green acknowledged the existence of objections and certain qualifications to the theory concerning the general good and obedience, while insisting on its general validity. (See *ibid.,* pp. 126-128 and 131-135.) Similar observations are made by Jouvenel (**On Power**, pp. 25-26; Br. ed.: **Power**, pp. 32-33); Simmel (Wolff, ed., **The Sociology of Georg Simmel**, p. 284); and Robert M. MacIver (**The Modern State** [Oxford at the Clarendon Press, 1926; London and New York: Oxford University Press, 1964], p. 154).

75. Watkins, ed., **Hume**, pp. 148-149.

76. *Ibid.*

77. Green, **Lectures . . .** , pp. 103 and 109.

78. *Ibid,.* p. 109.

79. Watkins, ed., **Hume**, p. 104.

80. See Austin, **Lectures . . .** , p. 293 and Rudlin, "Obedience, Political," p. 417.

81. Jouvenel, **On Power**, p. 355 (see also pp. 41-42); Br. ed.: **Power**, p. 301 (see also p. 45).

82. One of the conditions described by Mosca in which resistance to rulers was seen as impossible was "When the leaders of the governing class are the exclusive interpreters of the will of God or the will of the people and exercise sovereignty in the name of those abstractions in societies that are deeply imbued with religious beliefs or with democratic fanaticism . . ." (Mosca, **The Ruling Class**, p. 134.)

83. MacIver, **The Web of Government**, p. 76.

84. Jouvenel, **On Power**, p. 24; Br. ed.: **Power**, p. 32.

85. Goldhamer and Shils, "Power and Status," p. 173; Jouvenel, **Sovereignty**, p. 5; Pigors, **Leadership or Domination**, p. 311; Godwin, **Enquiry** . . . , vol. I, p. 250. Several sources of authority described by Hume clearly refer to ways in which the legitimacy of the ruler may be established. In addition to the supposed role of original contract, he discusses five other sources: (a) time ("long possession in any one form of government or succession of princes"), (b) present possession, (c) right of conquest, (d) right of succession, and (e) "positive laws" enacted by the legislature to fix a form of government or succession of princes. These sources, Hume stated, may appear in combinations and in varying degrees. (See Watkins, ed., **Hume**, pp. 106-113 and 197-198.)

86. Max Weber has distinguished three "pure types" of "ruling power, profane and religious, political and apolitical," on the basis of the type of legitimacy claimed by the ruling power. These are: (a) charismatic authority "a rule over men, whether predominantly external or internal, to which the governed submit because of their belief in the extraordinary quality of the specific *person*"), (b) traditionalist authority (domination resting upon "piety for what actually, allegedly, or presumably has always existed"), and (c) legal authority ("based upon an *impersonal* bond to the generally defined and functional 'duty of office,' " the official duty being fixed "by *rationally established* norms, by enactments, decrees, and regulations, in such a manner that the legitimacy of the authority becomes the legality of the general rule, which is purposely thought out, enacted, and announced with formal correctness"). (Gerth and Mills, eds., **From Max Weber**, pp. 294-301.)

87. MacIver, **The Web of Government**, p. 76.

88. Green, **Lectures** . . . , p. 101.

89. Watkins, ed., **Hume**, p. 150.

90. *Ibid.*

91. *Ibid.*, p. 155.

92. MacIver, **The Web of Government**, p. 76.

93. Godwin, **Enquiry** . . . , vol. II, p. 45; see also pp. 42-45.

94. Tolstoy, **The Kingdom of God is Within You**, U.S. ed., p. 302, Br. ed., p. 474.

95. Deutsch, "Cracks in the Monolith," p. 315.

96. MacIver, **The Web of Government**, p. 76.

97. Barnard, **The Functions of the Executive**, p. 167.

98. See Pigors, **Leadership or Domination**, p. 311, and Mosca, **The Ruling Class**, p. 53.

99. See Alexis de Tocqueville, **Democracy in America** (Trans. by George Lawrence, and ed. by J. P. Mayer; Garden City, N.Y.: Doubleday & Co., Anchor Books, 1969), p. 658.

100. Tolstoy, **The Kingdom of God is Within You**, U. S. ed., pp. 293-294; Br. ed., pp. 459-460. Arguing that English education increased Indian submission to the

colonial system, Gandhi wrote: "Culturally, the system of education has torn us from our moorings, our training has made us hug the very chains that bind us." (Quoted, Gene Sharp, **Gandhi Wields the Weapon of Moral Power** (Ahmedabad: Navajivan, 1960), p. 54.

101. See Barnard, **The Functions of the Executive**, p. 170.

102. See Sebastian de Grazia, The **Political Community: A Study of Anomie** (Chicago: University of Chicago Press, 1948), especially p. 177; Jouvenel, **On Power**, p. 11; Br. ed.: **Power**, p. 22; Wolff, ed., **The Sociology of Georg Simmel**, p. 193; Machiavelli, **The Discourses** . . . , vol. I, p. 496; Tocqueville, **Democracy in America**, pp. 257 and 701-702; and especially Erich Fromm, **Escape From Freedom** (New York: Holt Rinehart and Winston, 1961; Br. ed.: **The Fear of Freedom**, London: Routledge and Kegan Paul, 1961 [orig. 1942]).

103. Rousseau, "The Social Contract," p. 7.

104. Jouvenel, **On Power**, p. 20; Br. ed. **Power**, p. 29. See also Pigors, **Leadership or Domination**, p. 197. MacIver, **The Modern State**, p. 47; Tolstoy, **The Kingdom of God is Within You**, U.S. ed., pp. 276 and 294; Br. ed., pp. 434 and 460; and Mohandas K. Gandhi, **Hind Swaraj or Indian Home Rule** (Ahmedabad: Navajivan, 1958 [orig. 1909]), pp. 56-57.

105. This has not always been a characteristic of all political systems. For centuries, says Jouvenel, Rome had no permanent officials or standing army within its walls and only a few lictors (Jouvenel, **On Power**, p. 20; Br. ed.: **Power** p. 29). Montague also mentions the absence of State means of enforcement. (See his Introduction to Bentham, **A Fragment on Government**, p. 73.)

106. Jouvenel, **Sovereignty**, pp. 32-33.

107. See MacIver, **The Modern State**, p. 47.

108. Bertrand Russell, **Authority and the Individual: The Reith Lectures for 1948-1949** (New York: Simon & Schuster, 1949 and London: George Allen and Unwin, 1949), U.S. ed., p. 14: Br. ed., p. 30. See also MacIver, **The Web of Government**, p. 16, and Watkins, ed., **Hume**, p. 148.

109. Boetie, quoted in Leo Tolstoy, **The Law of Violence and the Law of Love** (Trans. by Mary Koutouzow Tolstoy; New York: Rudolph Field, 1948), p. 44; a slightly different wording appears in Boetie, **Anti-Dictator** (trans. Harry Kurz), p. 43.

110. Austin argued that "no conceivable motive will *certainly* determine to compliance, or no conceivable motive will render obedience inevitable." (Austin, **Lectures** . . . , vol. I, p. 90.)

111. Montague, "Introduction" to Bentham, **A Fragment on Government**, p. 74.

112. MacIver, **The Web of Government**, p. 76.

113. Jouvenel, **On Power**, p. 18; Br. ed.: **Power**, p. 27.

114. Rudlin, **"Obedience, Political,"** p. 417.

115. Russell, **Power**, p. 177; Br. ed., p. 183.

116. See, e.g., Tocqueville, **Democracy in America**, p. 139; Watkins, ed., **Hume**, pp. 155-156; Jouvenel, **Sovereignty**, p. 2; Russell, **Power**, pp. 117-118; Br. ed., p. 120.

117. See Austin, **Lectures** . . . , vol. I, p. 90; Jouvenel, **Sovereignty**, p. 33; and Deutsch, "Cracks in the Monolith," p. 314.

118. Austin insisted that ". . . every *forbearance* is *intended;* and is either the effect of an aversion from the consequences of the act forborne, or is the effect of a preference of that act. Consequently, every forbearance, like every act, is the

consequence of a desire." (Austin, **Lectures** . . . , p. 453.)

119. Jouvenel, **Sovereignty,** p. 33.

120. Mohandas K. Gandhi, **Young India,** 30 June 1920; quoted in Nirmal Kumar Bose, **Selections from Gandhi** (Ahmedabad: Navajivan, 1948), p. 116.

121. Austin, Lectures . . . , pp. 295-297.

122. Within a relationship of subordination, the exclusion of all spontaneity whatever is actually rarer than is suggested by such widely used popular expressions as 'coercion,' 'having no choice,' 'absolute necessity,' etc. Even in the most oppressive and cruel cases of subordination, there is still a considerable measure of personal freedom. We merely do not become aware of it, because its manifestation would entail sacrifices which we usually never think of taking upon ourselves. Actually, the 'absolute' coercion which even the most cruel tyrant imposes upon us is always distinctly relative. Its condition is our desire to escape from the threatened punishment or from other consequences ot our disobedience. More precise analysis shows that the super-subordination relation destroys the subordinate's freedom only in the case of direct physical violation. In every other case, this relationship only demands a price for the realization of freedom — a price, to be sure, which we are not willing to pay. It can narrow down more and more the sphere of external conditions under which freedom is clearly realized, but except for physical force [i.e. direct physical violation], never to the point of the complete disappearance of freedom." (Wolff, ed., **The Sociology of Georg Simmel,** p. 183.)

123. Austin: "Our desire of avoiding the evil which we might chance incur by disobedience makes us will the act which the command enjoins, makes us forbear from the act which the command forbids." (Austin, **Lectures** . . . , p. 453.)

Hobbes is prominent among those who have recognized the role of fear of the ruler's punishment in securing consent. The case "where a Sovereign Power is acquired by Force" occurs, he said, "when a man singly, or together by plurality of voyces, for fear of death, or bonds, do authorise all the actions of that Man, or Assembly, that hath their lives and liberty in his Power." (Hobbes, **Leviathan,**U.S. ed., p. 167; Br. ed., p. 152.)

124. Robert Michels, "Authority," **Encyclopedia of the Social Sciences** (New York: MacMillan, 1935), vol. II, p. 319.

125. Gandhi, **Young India,** 18 August 1920; quoted in Gandhi, **Non—Violent Resistance** (U.S. ed.: New York: Schocken Books, 1957; Indian ed.: **Satyagraha,** Ahmedabad, India: Navajivan, 1951), p. 157.

126. See MacIver, **The Web of Government,** p. 16; William Laud, quoted in Gerth and Mills, **Character and Social Structure,** p. 194; and Green, Lectures . . . , p. 126.

127. Austin, Lectures . . . , vol. I, pp. 295-296.

128. "Since, then, a government continues through the obedience of the people," argued Austin, "and since the obedience of the people is voluntary or free, every government continues through the consent of the people or the bulk of the political society." *(Ibid.,* vol. I, p. 296.)

129. *Ibid.,* vol. I, pp. 295-297.

130. Godwin, **Enquiry** . . . , vol. I, p. 145.

131. Adolf Hitler, **Mein Kampf** (New York: Reynal and Hitchcock, 1941), p. 388.

132. Austin, Lectures . . . , vol. I, p. 297.

133. *Ibid.,* pp. 296-297.

134. The nature of this disruption may vary considerably with the precise means used.

135. Harris, "Political Power," p. 6.

136. *Ibid.*, p. 8.

137. *Ibid.*, pp. 8-9.

138. Leo Tolstoy, "A Letter to a Hindu," in The Works of Tolstoy, vol. 21, **Recollections and Essays,** (London: Oxford University Press, Humphrey Milford, 1937), p. 427; Indian ed.: Kalidas Nag, **Tolstoy and Gandhi** (Patna, India: Pustak Bhandar, 1950), pp. 92-93.

139. Jouvenel, **Sovereignty,** p. 33.

140. *Ibid.*

141. Godwin, **Enquiry . . . ,** vol. I, pp. 145-146.

142. *Ibid.*, vol. I, p. 254.

143. "The moment the slave resolves that he will no longer be a slave, his fetters fall. He frees himself and shows the ways to others. Freedom and slavery are mental states. Therefore, the first thing is to say to yourself: 'I shall no longer accept the role of a slave. I shall not obey orders as such but shall disobey them when they are in conflict with my conscience.' " (Gandhi, **Harijan,** 24 February 1946; quoted in M. K. Gandhi, **Nonviolence in Peace and War,** vol. II [Ahmedabad, India: Navajivan, 1949], p. 10.)

144. "It is not so much British guns that are responsible for our subjection as our voluntary cooperation." (Gandhi, **Young India,** 9 February 1921; quoted in Bose, **Selections from Gandhi,** p. 116.)

145. "I believe, and everybody must grant, that no Government can exist for a single moment without the cooperation of the people, willing or forced, and if people suddenly withdraw their cooperation in every detail, the Government will come to a standstill." (Gandhi, **Young India,** 18 August 1920; quoted in Gandhi, **Non-violent Resistance,** p. 157; Indian ed.: **Satyagraha,** p. 157.

146. Quoted in Clarence Marsh Case, **Nonviolent Coercion: A Study in Methods of Social Pressure** (New York: Century Co., 1923), pp. 391-392.

147. Godwin, **Enquiry . . . ,** vol. I, pp. 253-254.

148. Gandhi, **Young India,** 16 June 1920; quoted in Gandhi, **Nonviolent Resistance,** pp. 114-115; Ind. ed.: **Satyagraha,** pp. 114-115.

149. Hillenbrand, **Power and Morals,** p. 5.

150. *Ibid.*, p. 10.

151. *Ibid.*, p. 22.

152. David Spitz, **Democracy and the Challenge of Power** (New York: Columbia University Press, 1958), p. viii.

153. Hillenbrand, **Power and Morals,** p. 5.

154. Jouvenel, **On Power,** p. 42; Br. ed.: **Power,** p. 45.

155. Maritain, **Man and the State,** U. S. ed., p. 64; Br. ed., pp. 58-59.

156. Boétie, *"Discours de la Servitude Volontaire,"* pp. 8-11; see also Boétie, **Anti-Dictator,** pp. 9-10.

157. Boétie, *"Discours de la Servitude Volontaire,"* pp. 12-14; see also, Boétie, **Anti-Dictator,** pp. 12-13.

158. The influence on Tolstoy, and through him on Gandhi is indisputable, as Tolstoy quotes from Boétie. The influence on Thoreau, however, I have not seen documented, although it is frequently stated to have been the case.

However, the close friendship between Emerson and Thoreau and the certainty of Emerson's familiarity with that essay makes it almost without doubt that Thoreau also knew it.

159. Machiavelli, **The Prince**, p. 77.

160. Machiavelli, **The Discourses . . .** , p. 254.

161. Gaetano Salvemini, **The French Revolution 1788-1792** (trans. by I. M. Rawson; New York: Henry Holt and Co., 1954, and London: Jonathan Cape, 1963), p. 162.

162. Thomas Hutchinson, ed., **The Complete Poetical Works of Percy Bysshe Shelley** (Oxford: Clarendon Press, 1904). p. 364. See esp. Shelley's "The Mask of Anarchy" in *ibid.)*

163. Jouvenel, **On Power**, p. 180; Br. ed.: **Power**, p. 154.

164. Jouvenel, **On Power**, p. 161; Br. ed.: **Power**, p. 138-139.

165. Tocqueville, **Democracy in America**, p. 139.

166. Austin, **Lectures . . .** , vol. I, p. 296.

167. Rousseau, "The Social Contract," p. 64.

168. Richard E. Neustadt, **Presidential Power: The Politics of Leadership** (New York and London: John Wiley and Sons, 1960), p. 7 (italics in the original).

169. *Ibid.,* pp. vii-viii.

170. *Ibid.,* pp. 36-37.

171. *Ibid.,* p. 41. The statement by A. Roosevelt Aide is from Johnathan Daniels, Frontier on the Potomac (New York: MacMillan, 1946), pp. 31-32.

172. *Ibid.,*p. 179.

173. *Ibid.,* pp. 26 and 32.

174. *Ibid.,* p. 9-10.

175. *Ibid.,* p. 9.

176. *Ibid.,* p. 163.

177. V. I. Lenin, "Political Report of the Central Committee of the Russian Communist Party (Bolsheviks)" delivered March 27, 1922, at the Eleventh Congress of the Russian Communist Party (Bolsheviks), **V. I. Lenin; Selected Works in Three Volumes** (New York: International Publishers, 1967), vol. III, pp. 692-693, and in Nikolai Lenin (sic), **The Essentials of Lenin in Two Volumes** (London: Lawrence and Wishart, 1947), vol. II, pp. 788-789.

178. Erich Eyck, **A History of the Weimar Republic**, vol. I. **From the Collapse of the Empire to Hindenburg's Election** (Cambridge, Mass.: Harvard University Press, 1962), p. 151.

179. S. William Halperin, **Germany Tried Democracy: A Political History of the Reich from 1918 to 1933** (Hamden, Conn. and London: Archon Books, 1946), p. 180.

180. Eyck, **A History of the Weimar Republic**, vol. I, pp. 151-152.

181. W. H. Crook, **The General Strike: A Study of Labor's Tragic Weapon in Theory and Practice** (Chapel Hill: University of North Carolina Press, 1931), p. 512.

182. D. J. Goodspeed, **The Conspirators: A Study in the Coup d'Etat** (New York: Viking Press, 1962; Toronto: Macmillan Co. of Canada, 1962), p. 131.

183. Crook, **The General Strike**, p. 515.

184. Halperin, **Germany Tried Democracy**, p. 179.

185. Goodspeed, **The Conspirators**, p. 130 and John W. Wheeler-Bennett, **The**

Nemesis of Power: The German Army in Politics, 1918-1945 (New York: St. Martin's Press, 1954 and London: Macmillan, 1953), p. 77.

186. Goodspeed, The Conspirators, p. 131.

187. Wheeler-Bennett, The Nemesis of Power, p. 79.

188. Goodspeed, The Conspirators, p. 211.

189. Jawaharlal Nehru, Toward Freedom (Rev. ed.; New York: The John Day Co., 1942), p. 249.

190. Quoted in D. G. Tendulkar, Mahatma: Life of Mohandas Karamachand Gandhi (New rev. ed.; Delhi: Publications Division, Ministry of Information and Broadcasting, Government of India, 1962), vol. VI, p. 88.

191. Government of India, India in 1930-31: A Statement Prepared for Presentation to Parliament in accordance with the requirements of the 26th section of the Government of India Act (5 & 6 Geo. V, Chapter 61) (Calcutta: Central Publication Branch, Government of India, 1932), pp. 80-81.

192. Alexander Dallin, German Rule In Russia, 1941-1945: A Study of Occupation Policies (New York: St. Martin's Press, 1957, and London: Macmillan, 1957), p. 218.

193. Ibid., p. 497.

194. Ibid., p. 516.

195. Quoted in ibid., p. 550.

196. Ibid., p. 663.

197. Ibid., p. 580.

198. Quoted in ibid., p. 498.

199. Tolstoy, The Law of Violence and the Law of Love, p. 47.

200. Watkins, ed., Hume, p. 198.

201. Hobbes' recognition of the power of disobedience apparently frightened him and encouraged his authoritarian view of government. In a discussion of "the poyson of seditious doctrines; whereof one is, That every private man is Judge of Good and Evill actions," Hobbes argues that this doctrine will lead men to decide to obey or disobey "the commands of the Commonwealth . . . as in their private judgements they shall think fit. Whereby the Common-wealth is distracted and Weakened." (Hobbes, Leviathan, U.S. ed., pp. 277-278; Br. ed., p. 249.)
Hobbes clearly placed obedience at the heart of political power and believed that disobedience therefore would lead to the ruler's collapse: "For the prosperity of a People ruled by an Artistocraticall, or Democraticall assembly, commeth not from Aristocracy, nor from Democracy, but from the Obedience, and Concord of the Subjects: nor do the people flourish in a Monarchy, because one man has the right to rule them but because they obey him. Take away in any kind of State, the Obedience, (and consequently the Concord of the People,) and they shall not only not flourish, but in a short time be dissolved. And they that go about by disobedience, to doe no more than reforme the Common-wealth, shall find they do thereby destroy it . . ."(Ibid., U.S. ed., pp. 291-292; Br. ed., p. 261.)

202. Watkins, ed., Hume, p. 115.

203. Hitler, Mein Kampf, pp. 872-873.

204. Gandhi, Harijan, 25 August 1940; quoted in Bose, Selections from Gandhi, p. 79.

205. Harris, "Political Power," p. 10.

206. **Vi Vill Oss et Land,** October 1940. Quoted in Hans Luihn, **De Illegale Avisene: Den Frie, Hemmilige Pressen i Norge Under Okkupasjonen** (Oslo and Bergen: *Universitetsforlaget,* 1960), p. 18.

207. Green, **Lectures . . . ,** p. 77.

208. Mosca, **The Ruling Class,** p. 53.

# 2

# Nonviolent Action: an Active Technique of Struggle

## INTRODUCTION

In political terms nonviolent action is based on a very simple postulate: people do not always do what they are told to do, and sometimes they do things which have been forbidden to them. Subjects may disobey laws they reject. Workers may halt work, which may paralyze the economy. The bureaucracy may refuse to carry out instructions. Soldiers and police may become lax in inflicting repression; they may even mutiny. When all these events happen simultaneously, the man who has been "ruler" becomes just another man. This dissolution of power can happen in a wide variety of social and political conflicts. The factory manager's power dissolves when the workers no longer cooperate. Political power disintegrates when the people withdraw their obedience and support. Yet the ruler's military equipment may remain intact, his soldiers uninjured, the cities unscathed, the factories and transport systems in full operational capacity, and the government buildings undamaged. But everything is changed. The human assistance which created and supported the regime's political power has been withdrawn. Therefore, its power has disintegrated.[1]

When people refuse their cooperation, withhold their help, and persist in their disobedience and defiance, they are denying their opponent the basic human assistance and cooperation which any government or hierarchical system requires. If they do this in sufficient numbers for long enough, that government or hierarchical system will no longer have power. This is the basic political assumption of nonviolent action.

# CHARACTERISTICS OF NONVIOLENT ACTION

Nonviolent action is a generic term covering dozens of specific methods of protest, noncooperation and intervention, in all of which the actionists conduct the conflict by doing—or refusing to do—certain things without using physical violence. As a technique, therefore, nonviolent action is not passive. It is *not* inaction. It is *action* that is nonviolent.

The issue at stake will vary. Frequently it may be a political one—between political groups, for or against a government, or, on rare occasions, between governments (as in imposition of embargoes or resistance to occupation). It may also be economic or social or religious. The scale and level of the conflict will also vary. It may be limited to a neighborhood, a city, or a particular section of the society; it may at other times range over a large area of a country or convulse a whole nation. Less often, more than one country and government may be involved. Whatever the issue, however, and whatever the scale of the conflict, nonviolent action is a technique by which people who reject passivity and submission, and who see struggle as essential, can wage their conflict without violence. Nonviolent action is not an attempt to avoid or ignore conflict. It is *one* response to the problem of how to *act* effectively in politics, especially how to wield power effectively.

## A. A special type of action.

It is widely assumed that all social and political behavior must be clearly either violent or nonviolent. This simple dualism leads only to serious distortions of reality, however, one of the main ones being that some people call "nonviolent" anything they regard as good, and "violent" anything they dislike. A second gross distortion occurs when people totally erroneously equate cringing passivity with nonviolent action because in neither case is there the use of physical violence.

Careful consideration of actual response to social and political conflict requires that all responses to conflict situations be initially divided into those of *action* and those of *inaction,* and not divided according to their violence or lack of violence. In such a division nonviolent action assumes its correct place as *one* type of *active* response. *Inaction,* which may include passivity, submission, cowardice and the like, will not detain us, for it has nothing to do with the nonviolent technique which is the subject of this book. By definition, nonviolent action cannot occur except by the replacement of passivity and submissiveness with activity, challenge and struggle.

Obviously, however, important distinctions must be made *within* the category of *action.* Here, too, a dichotomy into *violent* or *nonviolent* is too simple. Therefore, let us set up a rough typology of six major classes of the forms of action in conflicts, one of them nonviolent action, the technique with which we are concerned. This (rather crude) classification includes: 1) simple verbal persuasion and related behavior, such as conciliation; 2) peaceful institutional procedures backed by threat or use of sanctions: 3) physical violence against persons; 4) physical violence against persons plus material destruction; 5) material destruction only; and 6) the technique of nonviolent action. Obviously, each of these classes may itself be subclassified. People may shift back and forth between types of action, or back and forth between action and inaction. However, it is crucial to understand that the basic dichotomy of social and political behavior is between action and inaction, rather than between nonviolence and violence.

It is also important to see why and how nonviolent action as a technique differs from milder peaceful responses to conflicts, such as conciliation, verbal appeals to the opponent, compromise and negotiation. These responses may or may not be used with nonviolent action or with any of the other five kinds of action, but they should not be identified with the nonviolent technique as such. Conciliation and appeals are likely to consist of rational or emotional verbal efforts to bring about an opponent's agreement to something, while nonviolent action is not verbal—it consists of social, economic and political activity of special types. For example, asking an employer for a wage increase is an act of attempted simple verbal persuasion, but refusal to work until the wage increase is granted is a case of nonviolent action. Nor should nonviolent action be confused with compromise, which involves settling for part of one's objectives. Compromise is not a form of conflict or struggle, as is nonviolent action. As with violence, nonviolent action may or may not lead to a compromise settlement, depending on the issues,

# SIX CLASSES OF ACTION
# IN CONFLICTS

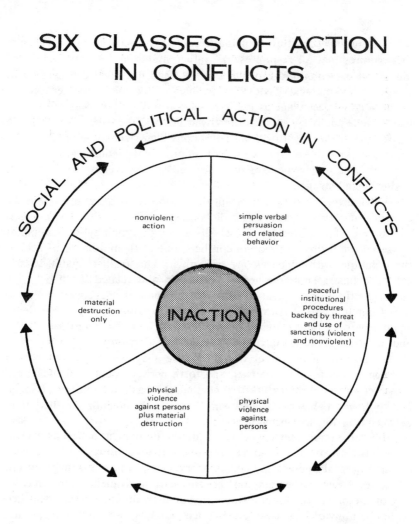

# CHART TWO

**PART ONE: POWER AND STRUGGLE**

power relationships, and the actionists' own decision. Similarly, negotiation is not a form of nonviolent action. Negotiation is an attempt at verbal persuasion, perhaps utilizing established institutional procedures, but always involving an implied or explicit threat of some type of sanction if an acceptable agreement is not reached. Negotiation could, therefore, precede a strike or a civil disobedience campaign, as it can a war. But such negotiation is an approach which must be distinguished from a strike, civil disobedience, or other form of nonviolent action.

Nonviolent action is so different from these milder peaceful responses to conflicts that several writers have pointed to the general similarities of nonviolent action to military war.[2] Nonviolent action is a means of combat, as is war. It involves the matching of forces and the waging of "battles," requires wise strategy and tactics, and demands of its "soldiers" courage, discipline, and sacrifice. This view of nonviolent action as a technique of active combat is diametrically opposed to the popular assumption that, at its strongest, nonviolent action relies on rational persuasion of the opponent, and that more commonly it consists simply of passive submission. Nonviolent action is just what it says: *action* which is nonviolent, not *inaction*. This technique consists, not simply of words, but of active protest, noncooperation and intervention. Overwhelmingly, it is group or mass action. Certain forms of nonviolent action may be regarded as efforts to persuade by action; others, given sufficient participants, may contain elements of coercion.

Another characteristic of nonviolent action which needs emphasis is that it is usually extraconstitutional; that is to say, it does not rely upon established institutional procedures of the State, whether parliamentary or nonparliamentary. However, it is possible to incorporate the technique into a constitutional system of government at various points, and it is also possible to use it in support of an established government under attack. Nonviolent action must not be confused with anarchism. That "no-State" philosophy has traditionally given inadequate thought to the practical problem of how to achieve such a society and to the need for realistic means of social struggle which differ in substance from those employed by the State.

## B. Motives, methods and leverages

The motives for using nonviolent action instead of some type of violent action differ widely. In some cases violence may have been rejected because of considerations of expediency, in others for religious, ethical, or moral reasons. Or there may be a mixture of motivations of various types.

Nonviolent action is thus not synonymous with "pacifism." Nor is it identical with religious or philosophical systems emphasizing nonviolence as a matter of moral principle. Adherents to some of these belief systems may see nonviolent action as compatible with their convictions and even as a fulfillment of them in conflicts. Adherents to certain other creeds which also emphasize nonviolence may, however, find this technique too "worldly" or "coercive" for them. Conversely, nonviolent action has often been practiced, and in a vast majority of the cases led, by nonpacifists who saw it only as an effective means of action. The popular idea that only pacifists can effectively practice nonviolent action —a view sometimes pressed with considerable conceit by pacifists themselves—is simply not true.

Furthermore, in many cases motivations for using nonviolent action have been mixed, practical considerations being combined with a *relative* moral preference for nonviolence (although violence was not rejected in principle). This type of mixed motivation is likely to become more frequent if nonviolent action is increasingly seen to have important practical advantages over violence.

It is frequently assumed that nonviolent actionists seek primarily to convert their opponent to a positive acceptance of their point of view. Actually, there is no standard pattern of priority for either changes in attitudes and beliefs, or policy and structural changes. Sometimes the nonviolent group may seek to change the opponent's attitudes and beliefs as a preliminary to changing his policies or institutions. Or the nonviolent action may be an expression of the determination of the members of the group not to allow the opponent to change their own attitudes or beliefs. Or the actions may be aimed primarily at changing policies or institutions or at thwarting the opponent's attempts to alter them, whether or not his attitudes and beliefs have first been changed (these cases appear to be in the majority). In still other cases, the nonviolent group may seek to change attitudes and policies simultaneously.

Nonviolent action may involve: 1) *acts of omission*—that is, people practicing it may refuse to perform acts which they usually perform, are expected by custom to perform, or are required by law or regulation to perform; 2) *acts of commission*—that is, the people may perform acts which they do not usually perform, are not expected by custom to perform, or are forbidden by law or regulation to perform; or 3) *a combination* of acts of omission and acts of commission.[3]

There are in the technique three broad classes of methods. 1) Where the nonviolent group uses largely symbolic actions intended to help persuade the opponent or someone else, or to express the group's disapproval and dissent, the behavior may be called *nonviolent protest and persuasion*. In this class are such demonstrations as marches, parades and vigils. These particular methods may be used either in an attempt to change opinions or to express disagreement, or both. 2) Where the nonviolent group acts largely by withdrawal or the withholding of social, economic, or political cooperation, its behavior may be described as *noncooperation*. This class contains three subclasses which include *social* noncooperation, *economic* noncooperation (economic boycotts and strikes), and *political* noncooperation. 3) Where the nonviolent group acts largely by direct intervention its action may be referred to as *nonviolent intervention*. The nonviolent group in this class clearly takes the initiative by such means as sit-ins, nonviolent obstruction, nonviolent invasion and parallel government. The technique may be applied by individuals, by small or large groups, and by masses of people.

Just as there is diversity among the many specific methods which constitute this technique, so also wide variation exists in the intensities of pressures and the types of leverage exerted by this technique. When successful, nonviolent action produces change in one of three broad ways, which we call *mechanisms of change*. In *conversion* the opponent reacts to the actions of the nonviolent actionists by finally coming around to a new point of view in which he positively accepts their aims. In *accommodation* the opponent chooses to grant demands and to adjust to the new situation which has been produced without changing his viewpoint. Where *nonviolent coercion* operates, change is achieved against the opponent's will and without his agreement, the sources of his power having been so undercut by nonviolent means that he no longer has control. These three mechanisms are discussed in detail in Chapter Thirteen.

To a degree which has never been adequately appreciated, the nonviolent technique operates by producing power changes. Both the relative power and the absolute power of each of the contending groups are subject to constant and rapid alterations. This power variability can be more extreme and occur more rapidly than in situations where both sides are using violence. As may be expected, the actionists seek continually to increase their own strength and that of their supporters. They will usually seek and gain assistance and active participation also from among the wider group affected by the grievances. In addition, the nature of nonviolent struggle makes it possible for the actionists also to win considerable support even in the camp of the opponent and among third parties. This potential is much greater than with violence. The ability to gain these types of support gives the nonviolent group a capacity to influence—and at times to regulate—*their opponent's* power, by reducing or severing the power of the opponent at its sources. Usually the results of these complex changes in the relative power positions of the contenders will determine the struggle's final outcome.

Nonviolent discipline must be viewed in the context of the mechanisms of change of this technique and the ways in which these power shifts are produced. The maintenance of nonviolent discipline in face of repression is not an act of moralistic naïveté. Instead, it contributes to the operation of all three mechanisms and is a prerequisite for advantageous power changes. As a consequence, nonviolent discipline can only be compromised at the severe risk of contributing to defeat. Other factors are, of course, highly important too, and it should not be assumed that maintenance of nonviolence will alone inevitably produce victory.

## C. Correcting misconceptions

It is widely assumed that nonviolent action must always take a very long time to produce victory, longer than violent struggle would take. This may be true at times, but not necessarily so, and at times the situation even seems reversed. Violent struggle may take many months or years to defeat the opponent, assuming that it eventually does so. In a variety of cases nonviolent struggle has won objectives in a very short time indeed. The 1766 repeal of the Stamp Act, which the American colonists resisted, came in a very few months. The 1920 Kapp *Putsch* in Germany was defeated in days. In 1942 Norwegian teachers within months defeated the Quisling regime's first effort at establishing a fascist Corporative State. In 1944 the dictators of El Salvador and Guatemala were ousted in a matter of days. Economic boycotts in American cities have often very quickly induced significantly increased hiring of Afro-Americans. The time taken to achieve victory depends on diverse factors —primarily on the strength of the nonviolent actionists.

By examining and correcting misconceptions about nonviolent action we are often able to bring out more sharply positive characteristics. 1) As has been pointed out above, this technique has nothing to do with passivity, submissiveness and cowardice; just as in violent action, these must first be rejected and overcome. 2) Nonviolent action is not to be equated with verbal or purely psychological persuasion, although it may use action to induce psychological pressures for attitude change; nonviolent action, instead of words, is a sanction and a technique of struggle involving the use of social, economic and political power, and the matching of forces in conflict. 3) Nonviolent action does not depend on the assumption that man is inherently "good"; the potentialities of man for both "good" and "evil" are recognized, including the extremes of cruelty and inhumanity. 4) People using nonviolent action do not have to be pacifists or saints; nonviolent action has been predominantly and successfully practiced by "ordinary" people. 5) Success with nonviolent action does not require (though it may be helped by) shared standards and principles, a high degree of community of interest, or a high degree of psychological closeness between the contending groups; this is because when efforts to produce voluntary change fail, coercive nonviolent measures may be employed. 6) Nonviolent action is at least as much of a Western phenomenon as an Eastern one; indeed, it is probably more Western, if one takes into account the widespread use of strikes and boycotts in the labor movement and the noncooperation struggles of subordinated nationalities. 7) In nonviolent action there is no assumption that the opponent will refrain from using violence against nonviolent actionists; the technique is designed to operate against violence when necessary. 8) There is nothing in nonviolent action to prevent it from being used for both "good" and "bad" causes, although the social consequences of its use for a "bad" cause may differ considerably from the consequences of violence used for the same cause. 9) Nonviolent action is not limited to domestic conflicts within a democratic system; it has been widely used against dictatorial regimes, foreign occupations, and even against totalitarian systems.

## D. A neglected type of struggle

Nonviolent action has not always brought full, or even partial, victory. People using nonviolent action have been defeated. It is no magic ritual. This is also true of violent action, however, including military struggle. No type of struggle guarantees short-term victory every time it is used. Failure in specific cases of nonviolent action, however, may be caused by weaknesses in a group employing the technique or in the strategy and tactics used—as may be the case in military action. If the group using nonviolent action does not as yet possess sufficient internal strength, determination, ability to act, and related qualities to make nonviolent action effective, then repetition of phrases and words like "nonviolence" will not save it. There is no substitute for genuine strength and skill in nonviolent action; if the actionists do not possess them sufficiently to cope with the opponent, they are unlikely to win. Considering the widespread ignorance of the nature and requirements of nonviolent action and the absence of major efforts to learn how to apply it most effectively, it is surprising that it has won any victories at all. Comparative studies are urgently needed of cases of "failure" and "success," and of possible ways to improve effectiveness.

It is clear, however, that the failures of nonviolent action do not adequately explain its widespread nonrecognition as a viable technique of struggle. This nonrecognition has taken several forms. One is a lack of attention to the history of nonviolent action. This technique has been widely used. It has a long history. At the moment of its use, its power and effectiveness have frequently been widely acknowledged; but once the particular case is over these characteristics are often forgot. Even the memory of them recedes. It is difficult to find good factual accounts of past nonviolent struggles.

The roots of this nonrecognition are hard to pinpoint, to separate one from the other and to trace to specific neglect. Suggested explanations can only be tentative at this stage of investigation. On a popular level it is easy to romanticize the more dramatic and heroic acts of violence for good causes, and the memory of such bravery has its influence on how the present is viewed, and therefore the past. Although nonviolent action may be equally heroic and dramatic, rarely do its deeds and heroes become romanticized as examples for future generations. There are also other, perhaps more fundamental, possible reasons for this nonrecognition. Some of the neglect of nonviolent struggle by historians may be rooted in their personal preconceptions and their acceptance of their society's assumption that violence is the only really significant and effective form of combat. In addition, where historians have been closely allied to established oppressive systems and ruling elites and have allowed that alliance to influence their writing, their neglect of these forms of struggle may be traced to consideration of the best interests of the ruling minority. The detailed recounting of forms of struggle usable by people who lack military weapons might be thought of as actual instruction in an antielitist technique which the people could use against their rulers. Furthermore, by recording effective continuing noncooperation, for example, the historian might cast aspersions on the established ruler and administration by implying that they were either inefficient or unpopular.

Anthropologists have revealed great cultural diversity among human societies, which include quite opposite attitudes and behaviors toward violence and nonviolence. Were it not for this diversity it would be difficult to avoid the conclusion that human nature is more violent than nonviolent. Many people accept this conclusion. Such a view influences not only what is done, but also how we interpret what happens. The conclusion that human beings are basically violent is, however, a distortion of reality, for in its assumptions Western civilization is biased toward violence. Indeed, when people in our society are confronted with situations in which violence obviously suffers from grave disadvantages and where significant evidence shows that nonviolent alternatives exist, a large number of people will still say that they *believe* violence to be necessary—a resort to conviction rather than evidence. This built-in bias toward violence may also contribute to the nonrecognition of the viability of nonviolent action.

There is one more possible explanation of the nonrecognition of nonviolent action as a significant political technique, a much simpler one. Why has not any new way of viewing the world been accepted earlier? Why, although apples had fallen from trees for centuries, did it remain for Newton to formulate the law of gravity? How is it that slavery could be accepted for many centuries as a right and necessary social institution? So one might ask similar questions about diverse approaches to understanding reality and viewing society. The explanation of the neglect and nonrecognition of nonviolent action—its practice, nature and potential—may be very similar to answers to these different questions.

In addition, until very recently no overall conceptual system existed to reveal relationships between diverse and apparently dissimilar historical events which are now grouped as cases of nonviolent action. We can now see, not simply a multitude of separate and unrelated events and forms of action, but one common technique of action. The resistance of Roman plebeians, the defiance of American colonials, the boycotting by Irish peasants, the strikes by workers of St. Petersburg, the fasts of Algerian nationalists, the civil disobedience by Gandhians, the refusal of Afro-Americans to ride buses in Montgomery, Alabama, and the arguments of students in Prague with Russian tank crews—all are different aspects of essentially the same type of behavior: nonviolent action. For the many forms of military struggle an overall conceptual tool has long existed, and this itself may have contributed to the detailed attention which wars have received. Attention to war has included historical and strategic studies which could help in future wars. But, until very recently, nonviolent action has had no comparable self-conscious tradition. Such a tradition would probably have brought attention to many of these neglected struggles and might well have provided knowledge to be used in new cases of nonviolent action.

There has been, then, little or no awareness of the history of nonviolent action, not only among the general public but also among future leaders of nonviolent struggles. Contrary to earlier assumptions, before undertaking his own campaigns Gandhi had a general knowledge of several important nonviolent struggles, especially in Russia, China and India; but even so he lacked the detailed knowledge that could have been gained from such conflicts.[4]

Another form of nonrecognition of nonviolent action is the general practice of unfairly comparing it with violence by using different standards of assessment for the two techniques. Sometimes when violence has had no chance of succeeding (even despite preparations), nonviolent action has been used, despite highly unfavorable conditions—including the usual lack of preparations, as in Czechoslovakia in 1968. Then when it failed, nonviolent action has later been criticized or condemned *as a whole* because its accomplishments were limited, slow to appear, or even absent. When violence fails, or when its achievements are limited or take time, *specific* inadequacies or factors are frequently blamed—not the technique itself. This rarely happens when nonviolent action is used, however. Rarely are the violent and nonviolent techniques carefully and fairly compared in terms of time, casualties, successes and failures (using specific criteria), adequacy of preparations, type of strategy, and the like. In cases where nonviolent action has produced partial or full successes, the tendency is to forget, minimize, or dismiss these as irrelevant. Full successes are sometimes written off, without careful analysis, as having been unique and without significance for future politics. This was the case with the downfall of the tsarist regime in Russia in 1917 and the collapse of the dictators of El Salvador and Guatemala in 1944. Who remembers these as victories won by nonviolent struggle? Where past struggles *are* remembered, their victories are forgotten or denied or minimized (as with the American colonists' struggles and the United States civil rights campaigns); or they are explained as having been unrelated to the nonviolent struggle or only partially so (as with the Gandhian struggles in India). Partial successes are often regarded as total failures —for example, the Ruhr struggle against the French and Belgian occupation in the period after World War I. In other cases, the nonviolent struggles may not be deliberately belittled, but greater attention may be paid to the less successful or less important violent struggles which preceded the nonviolent action (as in nineteenth-century Hungary) or which occurred alongside it (as in Nazi-occupied Norway).

Articulate opposition to the technique has often been based on misunderstanding and lack of information. Supposed "friends of nonviolent means"—such as some pacifists—have often by their own distortions and lack of knowledge discouraged others from taking this technique seriously. Generally, however, past nonviolent action has been ignored in contemplating how to face the conflicts of the future.

# ILLUSTRATIONS FROM THE PAST

Despite its widespread practice, nonviolent action has therefore remained an underdeveloped political technique. Very little deliberate effort has been given to increasing knowledge of its nature and how it works. Practically no research and planning have been carried out to promote its development and refinement. This is in sharp contrast to military war, guerrilla struggle, and the procedures of representative democracy. To date what we have in nonviolent action is essentially a raw, unrefined, intuitive technique—a type of struggle which still awaits efforts to increase its effectiveness and expand its political potential.

Nevertheless, in the past hundred years nonviolent action has risen to unprecedented political significance throughout the world. People using it have amassed major achievements. Higher wages and improved working conditions have been won. Old traditions and practices have been abolished. Government policies have been changed, laws repealed, new legislation enacted, and governmental reforms instituted. Invaders have been frustrated and armies defeated. An empire has been paralyzed, a seizure of power thwarted, and dictators overthrown. Sometimes, too, this technique has been used—as by Deep South segregationists—to block or delay changes and policies regarded by others as desirable and progressive.

## A. Some early historical examples

Much of the long history of nonviolent action has been lost for lack of interest in recording and recounting these struggles. Even existing historical accounts and other surviving information have not been brought together. The result is that a comprehensive history of the practice and development of the technique does not yet exist. Therefore, in this section we can only outline the history of nonviolent action in broad terms and illustrate it with more detailed sketches of a few especially interesting or significant cases. These were not necessarily influential in later struggles, for much of the use of this technique has been independent of earlier practice.

Nonviolent action clearly began early: examples go back at least to ancient Rome. In 494 B.C., for example, the plebeians of Rome, rather than murder the consuls in an attempt to correct grievances, withdrew from the city to a hill, later called "the Sacred Mount." There they remained for some days, refusing to make their usual contribution to the life of the city. An agreement was then reached pledging significant improvements in their life and status.[5] Theodor Mommsen offers an account of a similar Roman action in 258 B.C. The army had returned from battle to find proposals for reform blocked in the Senate. Instead of using military action, the army marched to the fertile district of Crustumeria, occupied "the Sacred Mount," and threatened to establish a new plebeian city. The Senate gave way.[6]

Although occasionally there are in the literature other references to instances of nonviolent action in the ancient Mediterranean world, they are not detailed; a few will be cited later as examples of specific methods of this technique. No systematic attempt has been made to locate and assemble early cases of nonviolent action, not only from Rome, but from a variety of civilizations and countries. Nonviolent action certainly occurred between Roman times and the late eighteenth century, when the case material becomes rich—for example, the Netherlands' resistance to Spanish rule from 1565 to 1576 is one very prominent such struggle—but we lack a coherent account of instances of nonviolent action during these centuries. This still remains to be written. Careful search from this perspective even in existing historical studies might reveal a great deal.

## B. The pre-Gandhian expansion of nonviolent struggle

We can, however, see that a very significant pre-Gandhian expansion of the technique took place from the late eighteenth to the early twentieth centuries. During this period the technique received impetus from four groups. The first consisted of nationalists (and others who were ruled from distant capitals) who found nonviolent action useful in resisting a foreign enemy or alien laws. The struggles of the American colonists before 1775 furnish highly important cases of such nonviolent resistance. In this period Daniel Dulany of Maryland, for example, advocated economic resistance in order to force Parliament to repeal offensive laws. In his proposals he urged the colonists to accept principles of action which are basic to this technique: "Instead of moping, and puling, and whining to excite Compassion; in such a Situation we ought with Spirit, and Vigour, and Alacrity, to bid Defiance to Tyranny, by exposing its Impotence, by making it as contemptible, as it would be detestable."[7]

Nationalist examples include the Hungarian resistance against Austria between 1850 and 1867 and the Chinese boycotts of Japanese goods in the early twentieth century. Both the American and the Hungarian struggles were extremely significant and effective, yet the degree to which the Americans won their demands and British power was immobilized by noncooperation is today not often fully recognized.[8] The non-violent Hungarian resistance led by Deák is largely forgotten and is even lacking, it is said, a good historian; while the earlier, very unsuccessful, violent resistance under Kossuth is remembered and idealized.

The second source of impetus in the development of the nonviolent technique in this period came from trade unionists and other social radicals who sought a means of struggle—largely strikes, general strikes and boycotts—against what they regarded as an unjust social system, and for the improvement of the condition of working men. An examination of the histories of the labor movement and of trade union struggles, and an awareness of the current use of such methods, quickly reveal the vast extent to which strikes and economic boycotts have been and are still used. Indeed, it was action based on awareness that withdrawal of labor was a powerful instrument of struggle which not only made possible improved wages and working conditions, but frequently also contributed to an extension of the right to vote, to the political power of working people, and to reform legislation. The significance of this frequently escapes us today, when people are often more conscious of the inconveniences to themselves which strikes may involve. However real these may often be, it has been fortunate both for the labor movement and for society as a whole that predominantly strikes and boycotts have been used to right economic grievances, instead of physical attacks on factory managers and owners, arson, riots, bombings and assassinations. Today these may seem unlikely tools for such ends, but this is a reflection of the degree to which violent means of struggle have in this area been replaced with nonviolent ones in order to induce the desired concessions in negotiations. Today it is also largely forgotten that nonviolent struggle in the form of general strike, for example, had its exponents among advocates of major political and economic change.

A third source of impetus in the development of the nonviolent technique on the level of ideas and personal example came from individuals such as Leo Tolstoy[9] in Russia and Henry David Thoreau[10] in the United States, both of whom wanted to show how a better society might be peacefully created.

Thoreau, for example, sketched in the political potentialities of disobedience of "immoral" laws. "Let your life be a counter-friction to stop the machine," he wrote. Speaking of disobedience and willingness to go to prison as a means of struggle against slavery in the United States, he continued: "A minority is powerless while it conforms to the majority; it is not even a minority then; but it is irresistible when it clogs by its whole weight." He also envisaged that such disobedience would be practiced by the ruler's agents: "When the subject has refused allegiance, and the officer has resigned his office, then the revolution is accomplished."[11]

Tolstoy's argument in his "A Letter to a Hindu"—that it was the submissiveness and cooperation of the Indians which made British rule of India possible—is known to have made a great impression on Gandhi. In terms of political impact, however, the use of nonviolent action against foreign rulers and by the labor movement was far more important than such men as Thoreau and Tolstoy.

A fourth group which contributed more or less  unconsciously to the pre-Gandhian development of nonviolent struggle were opponents of despotism which originated, not abroad, but in their own country. Their contribution may be seen most clearly in the defeated Russian Revolution of 1905. This case deserves detailed and careful research and analysis, and its lessons may be much more profound than the ones usually offered: that the "situation was not ripe," or that a full-scale violent revolution was needed.

## C. Early twentieth-century cases

A sense of reality and political substance can perhaps best be infused into the generalizations about the nature of nonviolent action and this sketchy historical survey by illustrating it with brief accounts of a few of the cases which have occurred in the twentieth century, beginning with the Russian Revolution of 1905.

**1. Russian Empire—1905–06**[12]      The Russian Empire, which had been long ruled by tsars who believed in their divine duty to govern, had been shaken by internal unrest and by humiliating defeats in the Russo-Japanese War. The years immediately before 1905 had already seen expressions of dissatisfaction among the peasants, workers, students and the intelligentsia. There had been more demands for representative government. Strikes by industrial workers had occurred.

In January 1905 thousands joined a peaceful march to the Winter Palace in St. Petersburg to present a mild petition to the Tsar. The guards fired into the crowd; over a hundred persons were killed and over three hundred wounded. The day became known as "Bloody Sunday." A predominantly nonviolent revolution followed spontaneously. There was violence, especially among the peasants, but the year-long struggle was largely expressed in a multitude of forms of nonviolent action, especially strikes. The major strikes, which repeatedly paralyzed St. Petersburg and Moscow and the railway and communications systems, were only the most obvious forms of resistance. (Many of these are described in later chapters.) Whole provinces and nationalities broke away from tsarist control and set up independent governments.

By October the country was paralyzed. The Tsar finally issued the October Manifesto, granting an elected legislature, with admittedly incomplete but nevertheless significant powers—something he had vowed never to do. The revolution, however, continued. Newspapers and magazines ignored censorship regulations. Trade unions made rapid growth. Councils (called *soviets)* became popular organs of parallel government and were much more representative than the established regime. There had already been limited mutinies among soldiers and sailors; the loyalty of troops wavered, and upon their obedience or large-scale mutiny depended in part the continued life or complete collapse of the regime. About two-thirds of the government troops were unreliable at this point, reports one historian.

During a widespread strike movement the Bolsheviks and Mensheviks succeeded in getting the Moscow *Soviet* to endorse a plan to transform the city's general strike, in early December 1905, into an armed rising. In face of this rebel violence, with their own lives in danger, the soldiers in Moscow largely obeyed orders. The violent rising was crushed. The regime made this victory for the tsar the beginning of a counteroffensive against the revolution. The strikers had also faced other problems, but major historians cite the defeat of the Moscow rising as the beginning of the end of the 1905 revolution.

Certain forms of struggle persisted into 1906. The downfall of the tsarist autocracy was, however, postponed until the predominantly nonviolent revolution of February 1917—which as in 1905 took the political parties espousing revolution by surprise.

Gandhi's struggles began in South Africa in 1906 against white supremacist oppression of Indians and continued in India after his return home in 1915 until his assassination in 1948. This historical contribution will be discussed shortly. It is important to note, however, that non-Gandhian contributions to the development of the technique of nonviolent action and its political potentialities continued even after Gandhi's struggles had begun.

**2. Berlin—1920**[13]    The rightist Kapp *coup d'état* (or *Putsch)* against the young Weimar Republic of Germany was defeated by nonviolent action. This action was launched in support of the legitimate government after that government had fled Berlin. These events—which took place without advance preparation or training—merit attention, even though the *coup* itself was rather amateurish and the improvised resistance something less than a perfect model. The case also illustrates the point that nonviolent action may be used to defend and preserve a regime or political system as well as to oppose it.

From the start the new Weimar Republic faced immense difficulties associated with the loss of the war: economic dislocation, military unrest, and attempts at revolution. In these circumstances, a right-wing promonarchist *coup d'état* was planned by Dr. Wolfgang Kapp and Lieutenant-General Freiherr Walter von Lüttwitz with the backing of General Erich von Ludendorff and various other army officers. On March 10, 1920, General Lüttwitz presented President Friedrich Ebert with a virtual ultimatum. This was rejected by the government, and it became apparent that a *Putsch* would be attempted. Minister of Defense Gustav Noske warned Lüttwitz that if orders were disobeyed and troops were used in an attempt to overthrow the Republic, the government would call a general strike. A meeting of generals showed that they were unwilling to use military force to defeat a rightist *Putsch*. They would not defend the Republic.

The same day—March 12—the Kappists, despite their limited preparations, began their march on Berlin. Police officers sided with the conspirators. There was grave doubt that government soldiers would fire on the advancing troops from the Baltic Brigades. The Ebert government abandoned Berlin without a fight, going first to Dresden and then to Stuttgart. Berlin was occupied on Saturday, March 13. The Kappists declared a new government. However, the *Länder* (states) were directed by the Ebert government to refuse all cooperation with the Kapp regime and to maintain contact only with the legal government.

When *Freikorps* (independent para-military units) troops occupied the offices of two progovernment newspapers on Sunday afternoon all Berlin printers went on strike. Other workers in Berlin by scores of thousands also spontaneously went on strike. Later that Sunday a call for a general strike against the *coup* was issued under the names of the members of the Executive Committee of the Social Democratic Party (S.P.D.) and the S.P.D. members of the Ebert Cabinet: "There is but one means to prevent the return of Wilhelm II: the paralysis of all economic life. Not a hand must stir, not a worker give aid to the military dictatorship. General Strike all along the line."[14] The general strike was supported by workers of all political and religious groups. (The Communists, however, had at first refused to support it.) No "essential services" were exempted. As described in Chapter One, the bureaucracy itself noncooperated. The

Kappist regime lacked money, and ordinary civil servants struck or otherwise refused to head ministries under Kapp, who was unable to obtain cooperation from the bureaucracy. Workers tried to influence the Kappist troops.

On the fifteenth of March the Ebert government rejected proposals for a compromise. The limited power of the occupiers of the Berlin government offices became more obvious. Some *Reichswehr* (German army) commanders resumed loyalty to the government. Leaflets entitled "The Collapse of the Military Dictatorship" were showered on Berlin from an airplane. The strike continued to spread despite severe threats and actual deaths by shooting. On the morning of the seventeenth the Berlin Security Police demanded Kapp's resignation.

Later that day, Kapp did resign and fled to Sweden, leaving General Lüttwitz as Commander-in-Chief. Bloody clashes took place in many towns. That evening most of the conspirators left Berlin in civilian clothes and Lüttwitz resigned from his new post. The next day the Baltic Brigades—now under orders of the Ebert government—marched out of Berlin but did not hesitate to shoot and kill some civilians who had jeered at them. The *coup* was defeated and the Weimar Republic preserved. The Ebert government faced continuing unrest, however, as bloody conflicts between government troops and an armed "Red" army in the Rhineland took many lives.

An authority on the *coup d'état,* Lieutenant Colonel D.J. Goodspeed, has pointed to one of the central lessons to be learned from the Kapp *Putsch:* after having seized the machinery of government, the conspirators must "obtain the required minimum of consent for their own administration."

The Kapp *putsch* is the episode where this question of popular support is seen at its clearest . . . to all intents and purposes the *coup* seemed to have succeeded. Yet it was broken, very largely because the people would not obey the new government.[15]

The distinguished German historian Erich Eyck has also concluded that "the strike . . . brought the *coup* of Kapp and company to an end after only four days. Since the regular tools of the state had been found wanting, only immediate intervention by the populace could have saved it so soon."[16]

**3. The Ruhrkampf—1923**[17]  The resistance to the Kapp *Putsch* was followed quickly by another very significant nonviolent struggle in support of legitimate government. This was the German resistance, in 1923,

to the French and Belgian occupation of the Ruhr. During this remarkable struggle, trade unionists, industrialists, German civil servants, officials and many other people refused to obey or cooperate with the
occupation regime. French repression was very severe.

Besides noncooperation, the situation was also complicated at certain
stages by various types of sabotage. And there were economic problems
for all of Germany. The country's economic situation was endangered
by the severance of the industrial and coal-mining belt from the rest of
Germany, as well as by the financing of the resistance by unsupported
paper money.

The *Ruhrkampf* has been widely regarded as a failure. However,
France found her ability to control the Ruhr and extract its resources
and products frustrated, expenses in the attempt exceeding the economic
gains. The French government fell, in part at least because of French
domestic revulsion over the severe repression practiced by its occupation
troops and officials. French troops evacuated the Ruhr after the German
government agreed to call off the passive resistance campaign. The suc-
cess-failure ratio seems to have been mixed for each side.

## D. Gandhi's contribution

It was Gandhi who made the most significant personal contribution
in the history of the nonviolent technique, with his political experiments
in the use of noncooperation, disobedience and defiance to control
rulers, alter government policies, and undermine political systems. With
these experiments the character of the technique was broadened and its
practice refined. Among the modifications Gandhi introduced were greater
attention to strategy and tactics, a more judicious use of the armory of
nonviolent methods, and a conscious association between mass political
action and the norm of nonviolence. For participants, however, this
association was not absolutist in character, and clearly most took part
because this technique was seen to offer effective action. As a result of
Gandhi's work the technique became more active and dynamic. With his
political colleagues and fellow Indians, Gandhi in a variety of conflicts
in South Africa and India demonstrated that nonviolent struggle could be
politically effective on a large scale.

Gandhi used his nonviolent approach to deal with India's internal
problems as well as to combat the British occupation of his country, and
he encouraged others to do likewise. One of the well-known local uses
of his *satyagraha* took place at Vykom in South India in 1924 and
1925; it was conducted by some of Gandhi's supporters to gain rights

for the untouchables. In this case there was a considerable attempt to change the attitudes and feelings of the orthodox Hindus. Gandhi's frequent exhortations on the need to convert, not coerce, the opponent were well implemented in this case. Emphasis on conversion is not usual in nonviolent action, however, nor is this case typical of the Gandhian struggles. However, it is significant precisely because of the attempt to convert the opponent group despite the extreme "social distance" between the Brahmans and the untouchables.

**1. Vykom—1924-25**[18]    In Vykom, Travancore, one of the states ruled by an Indian maharajah instead of the British, untouchables had for centuries been forbidden to use a particular road leading directly to their quarter because it passed an orthodox Brahman temple. In 1924, after consultations with Gandhi, certain high-caste Hindu reformers initiated action. Together with untouchable friends, this group walked down the road and stopped in front of the temple. Orthodox Hindus attacked them severely, and some demonstrators were arrested, receiving prison sentences of up to a year. Volunteers then poured in from all parts of India. Instead of further arrests, the Maharajah's government ordered the police to keep the reformers from entering the road. A cordon was therefore placed across it. The reformers stood in an attitude of prayer before it, pleading with police to allow them to pass. Both groups organized day and night shifts. The reformers pledged themselves to nonviolence and refused to withdraw until the Brahmans recognized the right of the untouchables to use the highway. As the months passed, the numbers of the reformers and their spirits sometimes rose and sometimes fell. When the rainy season came and the road was flooded, they stood by their posts, shortening each shift to three hours between replacements. The water reached their shoulders. Police manning the cordon had to take to boats.

When the government finally removed the barrier, the reformers declined to walk forward until the orthodox Hindus changed their attitude. After sixteen months the Brahmans said: "We cannot any longer resist the prayers that have been made to us, and we are ready to receive the untouchables." The case had widespread reverberations throughout India, it is reported, assisting in the removal of similar restrictions elsewhere and strengthening significantly the cause of caste reform.

**2. Gandhi's theory of power**    Gandhi is better known, however, for his struggles against British domination. In these struggles he operated on the basis of a view of power and avowedly based his newly developed approach to conflict—*satyagraha*—upon a theory of power: "In politics, its use is based upon the immutable maxim that government of the people is possible only so long as they consent either consciously or unconsciously to be governed."[19] This constituted the basic principle of his grand strategy.

In Gandhi's view, if the maintenance of an unjust or nondemocratic regime depends on the cooperation, submission and obedience of the populace, then the means for changing or abolishing it lies in the noncooperation, defiance and disobedience of that populace. These, he was convinced, could be undertaken without the use of physical violence, and even without hostility toward the members of the opponent group. In *Hind Swaraj or Indian Home Rule,* an early pamphlet written in 1909, Gandhi expressed his theory of control of political power in a passage addressed to the British rulers:

> You have great military resources. Your naval power is matchless. If we wanted to fight with you on your own ground, we should be unable to do so, but if the above submissions be not acceptable to you, we cease to play the part of the ruled. You may, if you like, cut us to pieces. You may shatter us at the cannon's mouth. If you act contrary to our will, we shall not help you; and without our help, we know that you cannot move one step forward.[20]

A resolution drafted by Gandhi, approved by the All-India Working Committee of the Indian National Congress (the nationalist party), and passed by public meetings on the Congress-declared Independence Day, January 26, 1930, contained this statement on noncooperation and the withdrawal of voluntary submission to the British *Raj:*

> We hold it to be a crime against man and God to submit any longer to a rule that has caused this fourfold disaster to our country. We recognize, however, that the most effective way of gaining our freedom is not through violence. We will therefore prepare ourselves by withdrawing, so far as we can, all voluntary association from the British Government, and will prepare for civil disobedience, including nonpayment of taxes. We are convinced that if we can but withdraw our voluntary help and stop payment of taxes without doing violence, even under provocation, the end of this inhuman rule is assured.[21]

Later that same year, Gandhi, at the request of the Indian National Congress, launched a movement of noncooperation and disobedience for the attainment of *swaraj, i.e.,* "self-rule." This campaign was based upon the above theory, the seditious nature of which Gandhi had nearly ten years earlier openly avowed.

> . . . sedition has become the creed of the Congress. Every noncooperator is pledged to preach disaffection towards the Government established by law. Noncooperation, though a religious and strictly moral movement, deliberately aims at the overthrow of the Government, and is therefore legally seditious in terms of the Indian Penal Code.[22]

This withdrawal of support, Gandhi said, should be in proportion to "their ability to preserve order in the social structure" without the assistance of the ruler.[23] The way to control political power therefore became, in his view, "to noncooperate with the system by withdrawing all the voluntary assistance possible and refusing all its so-called benefits."[24] On this basis he had formulated *satyagraha*.

While he sought to convert the British, Gandhi had no illusions that there could be an easy solution without struggle and the exercise of power. Just before the beginning of the 1930-31 civil disobedience campaign he wrote to the Viceroy:

> It is not a matter of carrying conviction by argument. The matter resolves itself into one of matching forces. Conviction or no conviction, Great Britain would defend her Indian commerce and interests by all the forces at her command. India must consequently evolve force enough to free herself from that embrace of death.[25]

It was by no means inevitable that the Indian struggle would be nonviolent, and there are strong indications that in the absence of Gandhi's alternative grand strategy the terrorists would probably have carried the day. (This seems so despite the fact that nonviolent resistance played a significant role in the analyses and actions of Indian nationalists *before* Gandhi.)

Ranganath R. Diwakar, a participant in the independence struggle and author of several books on Gandhi's *satyagraha,* has written:

> In fact, if Gandhiji had not been there to guide and lead India, awakened and conscious as she was, she would certainly have adopted the usual methods of armed revolt against her alien oppressors. . . . it would have been inevitable. . . . A choice had to be made and at the psychological moment Gandhiji presented this unique weapon of satyagraha.[26]

Even after Gandhi's program of action had been accepted by the Indian National Congress and mass nonviolent campaigns had been launched, the terrorists continued to act, and there was wide support for advocates of violent revolution, especially for Subhas Chandra Bose, who was even elected president of the Congress in 1939. In 1928 Jawaharlal Nehru was still in favor of a violent war of independence. Contrary to many sentimental comments by both Indians and Westerners, this was the political context within which Gandhi's grand strategy was adopted and within which Gandhi formulated a series of nonviolent campaigns. One of these, the 1930-31 independence campaign, which began with the famous Salt March, remains a classic example of a nationwide nonviolent struggle.

**3. India—1930-31**[27]    For the 1930 campaign Gandhi formulated a program of political demands and a concrete plan for nonviolent rebellion, including civil disobedience. Pleas to the Viceroy produced no concessions.

Focusing initially on the Salt Act (which imposed a heavy tax and a government monopoly), Gandhi set out with disciples on a twenty-six day march to the sea to commit civil disobedience by making salt. This was the signal for mass nonviolent revolt throughout the country. As the movement progressed, there were mass meetings, huge parades, seditious speeches, a boycott of foreign cloth, and picketing of liquor shops and opium dens. Students left government schools. The national flag was hoisted. There were social boycotts of government employees, short strikes *(hartals),* and resignations by government employees and Members of the Legislative Assembly and Councils. Government departments were boycotted, as were foreign insurance firms and the postal and telegraph services. Many refused to pay taxes. Some renounced titles. There were nonviolent raids and seizures of government-held salt, and so on.

The government arrested Gandhi early in the campaign. About one hundred thousand Indians (including seventeen thousand women) were imprisoned or held in detention camps. There were beatings, injuries, censorship, shootings, confiscation, intimidation, fines, banning of meetings and organizations, and other measures. Some persons were shot dead. During the year the normal functioning of government was severely affected, and great suffering was experienced by the resisters. A truce was finally agreed on, under terms settled by direct negotiations between Gandhi and the Viceroy.

Although concessions were made to the nationalists, the actual terms favored the government more than the nationalists. In Gandhi's view it was more important, however, that the strength thus generated in the Indians meant that independence could not long be denied, and that by having to participate in direct negotiations with the nonviolent rebels, the government had recognized India as an equal with whose representatives she had to negotiate. This was as upsetting to Winston Churchill as it was reassuring to Gandhi.

Jawaharlal Nehru, who was later to become Prime Minister of independent India, was no believer in an ethic of nonviolence or Gandhi's philosophy or religious explanations. However, like many other prominent and unknown Indians, he became a supporter of Gandhi's nonviolent "grand strategy" for obtaining a British evacuation from India, and he spent years in prison in that struggle. Nehru wrote in his autobiography:

> We had accepted that method, the Congress had made that method its own, because of a belief in its effectiveness. Gandhiji had placed it before the country not only as the right method but as the most effective one for our purpose . . . .
>
> In spite of its negative name it was a dynamic method, the very opposite of a meek submission to a tyrant's will. It was not a coward's refuge from action, but a brave man's defiance of evil and national subjection.[28]

### E. Struggles against Nazis

Independent of the continuing Gandhian campaigns, significant nonviolent struggles under exceedingly difficult circumstances also emerged in Nazi-occupied Europe. Almost without exception these operated in the context of world war and always against a ruthless enemy. Sometimes the nonviolent forms of resistance were closely related to parallel violent resistance; occasionally they took place more independently. Often the nonviolent elements in the resistance struggles were highly important, sometimes even overshadowing the violent elements in the resistance.

Nonviolent resistance in small or large instances took place in a number of countries but was especially important in the Netherlands,[29] Norway[30] and, probably to a lesser degree, in Denmark.[31] In no case does there appear to have been much if anything in the way of special knowledge of the technique, and certainly no advance preparations or training. The cases generally emerged as spontaneous or improvised efforts to "do something" in a difficult situation. Exceptions were certain strikes in the Netherlands which the London-based government-in-exile requested in order to help Allied landings on the continent.

**1. Norway—1942**[32]     The Norwegian teachers' resistance is but one of these resistance campaigns. During the Nazi occupation, the Norwegian fascist "Minister-President," Vidkun Quisling, set out to establish the Corporative State on Mussolini's model, selecting teachers as the first "corporation." For this he created a new teachers' organization with compulsory membership and appointed as its Leader the head of the *Hird*, the Norwegian S. A. (storm troopers). A compulsory fascist youth movement was also set up.

The underground called on the teachers to resist. Between eight thousand and ten thousand of the country's twelve thousand teachers wrote letters to Quisling's Church and Education Department. All signed their names and addresses to the wording prescribed by the underground for the letter. Each teacher said he (or she) could neither assist in promoting fascist education of the children nor accept membership in the new teachers' organization.

The government threatened them with dismissal and then closed all schools for a month. Teachers held classes in private homes. Despite censorship, news of the resistance spread. Tens of thousands of letters of protest from parents poured into the government office.

After the teachers defied the threats, about one thousand male teachers were arrested and sent to concentration camps. Children gathered and sang at railroad stations as teachers were shipped through in cattle cars. In the camps, the Gestapo imposed an atmosphere of terror intended to induce capitulation. On starvation rations, the teachers were put through "torture gymnastics" in deep snow. When only a few gave in, "treatment" continued.

The schools reopened, but the teachers still at liberty told their pupils they repudiated membership in the new organization and spoke of a duty to conscience. Rumors were spread that if these teachers did not give in, some or all of those arrested would be killed. After difficult inner wrestling, the teachers who had not been arrested almost without exception stood firm.

Then, on cattle car trains and overcrowded steamers, the arrested teachers were shipped to a camp near Kirkenes, in the Far North. Although Quisling's Church and Education Department stated that all was settled and that the activities of the new organization would cease, the teachers were kept at Kirkenes in miserable conditions, doing dangerous work.

However, their suffering strengthened morale on the home front and posed problems for the Quisling regime. As Quisling once raged at the teachers in a school near Oslo: "You teachers have destroyed everything for me!" Fearful of alienating Norwegians still further, Quisling finally ordered the teachers' release. Eight months after the arrests, the last teachers returned home to triumphal receptions.

Quisling's new organization for teachers never came into being, and the schools were never used for fascist propaganda. After Quisling encountered further difficulties in imposing the Corporative State, Hitler ordered him to abandon the plan entirely.

**2. Berlin—1943**     It is widely believed that once the "Final Solution," the annihilation of Europe's Jews, was under way, no nonviolent action to save German Jews occurred and that none could have been effective. This belief is challenged by an act of nonviolent defiance by the non-Jewish wives of arrested Berlin Jews. This limited act of resistance occurred in the midst of the war, in the capital of the Third Reich, toward the end of the inhuman effort to make Germany free of Jews—all highly unfavorable conditions for successful opposition. The defiance not only took place, but was completely successful, even in 1943. The following account is by Heinz Ullstein, one of the men who had been arrested; his wife was one of the women who acted:

> The Gestapo were preparing for large-scale action. Columns of covered trucks were drawn up at the gates of factories and stood in front of private houses. All day long they rolled through the streets, escorted by armed SS men. . . . heavy vehicles under whose covers could be discerned the outlines of closely packed humanity . . . On this day, every Jew living in Germany was arrested and for the time being lodged in mass camps. It was the beginning of the end.
>
> People lowered their eyes, some with indifference, others perhaps with a fleeting sense of horror and shame. The day wore on, there was a war to be won, provinces were conquered, "History was made," we were on intimate terms with the millennium. And the public eye missed the flickering of a tiny torch which might have kindled the fire of general resistance to despotism. From the vast collecting centers to which the Jews of Berlin had been taken, the Gestapo sorted out those with "Aryan kin" and concentrated them in a separate prison in the Rosenstrasse. No one knew what was to happen to them.
>
> At this point the wives stepped in. Already by the early hours of the next day they had discovered the whereabouts of their husbands and as by common consent, as if they had been summoned, a crowd

of them appeared at the gate of the improvised detention center. In vain the security police tried to turn away the demonstrators, some 6,000 of them, and to disperse them. Again and again they massed together, advanced, called for their husbands, who despite strict instructions to the contrary showed themselves at the windows, and demanded their release.

For a few hours the routine of a working day interrupted the demonstration, but in the afternoon the square was again crammed with people, and the demanding, accusing cries of the women rose above the noise of the traffic like passionate avowals of a love strengthened by the bitterness of life.

Gestapo headquarters was situated in the Burgstrasse, not far from the square where the demonstration was taking place. A few salvoes from a machine gun could have wiped the women off the square, but the SS did not fire, not this time. Scared by an incident which had no equal in the history of the Third Reich, headquarters consented to negotiate. They spoke soothingly, gave assurances, and finally released the prisoners.[33]

## F. Latin American civilian insurrections

Latin America is more famous for its political violence than for nonviolent action. This may be an unbalanced view. There have apparently been a large number of instances in Latin America of general strikes and several cases of nonviolent civilian insurrections. For example, within a few weeks in 1944 two Central American dictators, in El Salvador and Guatemala, fell before massive civil resistance. These cases are especially important because of the rapidity with which the nonviolent action destroyed these entrenched military dictatorships. Attention here is focused on the Guatemalan case.

**1. Guatemala—1944**[34]    With the help of the secret police General Jorge Ubico had ruled Guatemala since 1931. Ubico was extolled in some U.S. magazines as a "road-and-school dictator"; the men who had faced his political police knew better. *Time* magazine called him an admirer of Hitler's 1934 blood purge, and quoted Ubico: "I am like Hitler, I execute first and give trial afterwards . . ."[35]

During World War II many U.S. troops were in Guatemala, which had joined the Allies. The Americans there promoted ideas of democracy for which, they said, the war was being fought. These appealed especially to Guatemalan students and young professional men. Other changes were undermining Ubico's position. Seizure of German-owned coffee *fincas* (plantations) in 1942 removed some of his supporters. Domestic issues were causing unrest, both among workers and within the business community. The dictator of nearby El Salvador, Martinez, had fallen a few weeks previously in the face of widespread nonviolent resistance. That proved to be a dangerous and contagious example. Action began in Guatemala, mildly—at first.

In late May 1944 forty-five lawyers asked the removal of the judge who tried most political opponents of the regime brought before a civil court. Ubico asked for specific charges against the judge. Surprisingly, one newspaper was allowed to publish them.

On the day prior to the annual parade of teachers and schoolchildren in tribute to the dictator, two hundred teachers petitioned Ubico for a wage increase. Those who drafted the petition were arrested and charged with conspiracy against the social institutions of the supreme government. The teachers replied with a boycott of the parade; they were fired.

On June 20 a manifesto announced the formation of the Social Democrat Party and called for opposition parties, social justice, lifting of the terror, and hemispheric solidarity. Students petitioned for university autonomy, rehiring of two discharged teachers and release of two imprisoned law students. Unless the demands were granted within twenty-four hours, they threatened a student strike.

Ubico declared a state of emergency. He called the opposition "nazifascist." Fearful, many student leaders sought asylum in the Mexican Embassy. However, young lawyers and professional men refused to submit to intimidation, and supported the students. On June 23 the schoolteachers went on strike.

Ubico had once said that if three hundred respected Guatemalans were to ask him to resign he would do so. On June 24 two men delivered the *Memorial de los 311* to Ubico's office. The three hundred and eleven prominent signers had risked their lives. The document explained the reasons for unrest, asked effective constitutional guarantees, and suspension of martial law. The same day, students marched past the U.S. Embassy and emphasized reliance on nonviolent means. Officials seemed surprised at the form of this demonstration. A peaceful meeting that evening demanded Ubico's resignation. Later that night, however, police beat and arrested hundreds at a neighborhood religious and social celebration. Some blamed "drunken bandits, previously coached by the police"; others pointed to clashes between persons shouting anti-Ubico slogans and the dictator's strong-arm men.

The next day the foreign minister summoned to the National Palace the two men who had delivered the *Memorial de los 311* —Carbonell and Serrano. The ex-head of the secret police joined the meeting. Simultaneously, a demonstration took place before the National Palace; against it the government massed platoons of soldiers, cavalry, tanks, armored cars, machine guns, and police armed with guns and tear-gas bombs. Carbonell and Serrano were asked to "calm the people." Although all meetings had been banned, the men were permitted to meet with other "leaders" of the movement to seek a solution to the crisis.

That afternoon women dressed in deep mourning prayed for an end to the night's brutalities at the Church of San Francisco in the center of Guatemala City. Afterward they formed an impressive silent procession; the cavalry charged and fired into the crowd. An unknown number were wounded and one, María Chincilla Recinos, a teacher, was killed. She became the first martyr. ". . . the mask had been torn from the Napoleonic pose, revealing Ubico and his regime standing rudely on a basis of inhumanity and terror."[36]

Guatemala City responded with a silent paralysis. The opposition broke off talks with the government. Workers struck. Businessmen shut stores and offices. It was an economic shutdown. Everything closed. The streets were deserted.

After attempts at a new parley failed, at Ubico's request the diplomatic corps arranged a meeting that afternoon between the opposition and the government. The delegates told Ubico to his face that during his rule "Guatemala has known nothing but oppression." Ubico insisted: "As long as I am president, I will never permit a free press, nor free association, because the people of Guatemala are not ready for a democracy and need a strong hand."[37] The possibility of Ubico's resigning and the question of a succession were discussed. The delegates were to sample public opinion.

The opposition later reported to Ubico by letter the unanimous desire of the people that he resign. They again demanded the lifting of martial law, freedom of press and association, and an end to attacks on the people. Petitions and messages from important people poured into the palace; they also asked Ubico to resign. The silent economic shutdown of Guatemala City continued. The dictator's power was dissolving.

On July 1 Ubico withdrew in favor of a triumvirate of generals. Immediate and unaccustomed political ferment followed. Labor and political organizations mushroomed, and exiles returned. General Ponce, one of the triumvirate, tried to install himself in Ubico's place. In October he faced another general strike and a student strike and was ousted by a *coup d'état*. Difficult times were still ahead.

The victory over Ubico was not well utilized to establish democracy. But it had been a victory, both for the people and for their type of struggle. Mario Rosenthal writes:

> Energetic and cruel, Jorge Ubico could have put down an armed attack . . . He could have imposed his will on any group of disgruntled, military or civilian, and stood them up against a wall. But he was helpless against civil acts of repudiation, to which he responded with violence, until these slowly pushed him into the dead-end street where all dictatorships ultimately arrive: kill everybody who is not with you or get out.[38]

> The movement that brought Waterloo to Guatemala's Napoleon was, fittingly, a peaceful, civilian action; the discipline, serenity and resignation with which it was conducted made it a model of passive resistance.[39]

Rosenthal also paid tribute to the intelligence with which it was directed and to the solidarity shown by Guatemalans of all social classes, and ethnic and political backgrounds.

## G. Risings against Communist regimes

Nonviolent forms of struggle have also emerged in several Communist-ruled countries. While always producing something less than total success and sometimes obvious defeat, these predominantly spontaneous corporate acts of defiance and resistance have sometimes shaken the regime to its core. The largely nonviolent East German Rising of June 1953 is a clear case in point.[40] During the Hungarian Revolution of 1956–57 the great variety of methods of nonviolent action applied, under severe conditions—methods such as the general strike, massive demonstrations, and the shifting of loyalty from the old government to the incipient parallel government of the workers' councils—had a powerful impact, and together they constituted an extremely important component in the total combat strength. The general strike was able to continue in Budapest for some time after the Russians had crushed the military resistance. Today it is often forgotten that nonviolent methods of struggle were very important in the Hungarian Revolution.[41]

**1. Vorkuta—1953**[42]    There was also a significant wave of strikes in the prison labor camps, especially among political prisoners, in the Soviet

Union itself in 1953.[43] In some of these there was a great deal of violence. In all there was repression, though apparently it was less severe where the prisoners were predominately nonviolent. Perhaps the most important of these strikes was at Vorkuta.

Strikes against poor conditions had long been considered among the 250,000 political prisoners in the coal-mining camps at Vorkuta. The decision was precipitated just after Stalin's death in 1953 by the announcement of the M.V.D. (Ministry of Internal Affairs) at Vorkuta that political prisoners ought not to expect an amnesty, as their liberation would jeopardize State security.

Many waverers then cast their lot with those advocating nonviolent resistance; by the end of May, strike committees had been secretly established in several camps. They were mainly composed of three groups of prisoners: Leninist students, anarchists, and the *Monashki* (a postrevolutionary pacifist Christian group resembling the early Quakers), as well as some prisoners representing no group.

The fall of Beria, the head of the secret police, while the prisoners were organizing encouraged more waverers. Strike committees were set up in coal-mining pits where they worked. It was agreed that the strike was to demand abolition of the camps and change of the prisoners' status to that of free colonists under contract. Before the strike began the central leadership was arrested and removed to Moscow. A new central strike committee was elected.

On July 21 many prisoners remained in their barracks, refusing to work. They insisted on presenting their demands to the general who was commandant of all the Vorkuta camps. They did so two days later, after thirty thousand had joined the strike. After the demands were presented the general made a long speech containing vague promises and specific threats.

A week passed without decisive action; no clear orders came from Moscow. Food would continue only while existing supplies lasted, it was announced. A strike leaflet appeared by the thousands of copies, urging self-reliance to gain freedom and the strike as the only possible means of action. Sympathetic soldiers helped to spread these and to maintain contacts between the camps. Twenty big pits were shut down.

Russian-speaking troops were then withdrawn and replaced by soldiers from Far Eastern sections of the Soviet Union, who did not speak Russian. With the strike at its peak in early August, the State Prosecutor arrived with several generals from Moscow and offered minor concessions: two letters home a month (instead of two a year), one visitor a year, and removal of identification numbers from clothes and iron bars from barracks windows.

In an open letter the strike leadership rejected these. The Prosecutor spoke at the camps, promising better food, higher pay, shorter shifts. Only a few wavered. The Strike Committee leaders went to an interview with the commanding general—but never returned. Some strikers were shot.

After the prisoners had held out for over three months the strike finally ended in the face of food and fuel shortages. However, considerable material improvements resulted. A spokesman of the International Commission on Concentration Camp Practices declared that the strike action in this and other camps was one of the most important factors in the improvement in the lot of the political prisoners.

## H. American civil rights struggles

In the United States in the mid-1950s there emerged among Afro-Americans and civil rights workers a very significant, large, and reasonably effective movement of nonviolent action against segregation and discrimination against Afro-Americans. The nonviolent action took a variety of forms—bus boycotts, various economic boycotts, massive demonstrations, marches, sit-ins, freedom rides and others. This movement dates from the Montgomery bus boycott, which remains significant despite changes in resistance methods in recent years.

**1. Montgomery, Alabama—1955-56**[44]     On December 1, 1955, four Negroes in Montgomery were asked, as was usual, to give up their bus seats to newly boarded whites and stand. Three complied, but Mrs. Parks, a seamstress, refused.

A one-day boycott of the buses on December 5 in protest against her arrest was nearly 100 percent effective. It was decided to continue the boycott until major reforms were made. Evening mass meetings in churches overflowed. The response, in numbers and spirit, exceeded all hopes.

Negroes walked, took taxis, and shared rides, but stayed off the buses. A new spirit of dignity and self-respect permeated the Negro community. The whites were confronted by qualities they had not believed the Negroes possessed. The aim became improvement of the whole community. The appeal was to Christian love. The young Rev. Martin Luther King, Jr., and his co-workers found themselves thrust into leadership and international prominence.

Negotiations failed. The use of taxis at reduced fares was prohibited.

A car pool of three hundred vehicles was organized. Money began to pour in, and a fleet of over fifteen new station wagons was added. Many Negroes preferred to walk to express their determination.

Unfounded rumors were spread about the movement's leaders, along with false reports of a settlement. Negro drivers (including Dr. King) were arrested for minor, often imaginary, traffic violations. Police intimidation became common. Over thirty threats a day reached the leaders. King's home was bombed; Negroes nearly broke into violence. Another home was bombed. Then nearly one hundred Negro leaders were arrested, charged with violating an antiboycott law.

Fear, long known by Southern Afro-Americans, was cast off. Many went to the sheriff's office, hoping to be among those "wanted." The trial of the arrested leaders, which received world attention, became a testimony of fearlessness and a recounting of grievances. The movement gained new momentum. On June 4 the Federal District Court, acting on a suit filed by the Negroes, declared the city bus segregation laws to be unconstitutional, but the city appealed. The bus protest continued, now to bring a full end to bus segregation. Insurance policies on the station wagons were canceled; a London firm issued new policies. City officials declared the car pool illegal. The same day, November 13, the United States Supreme Court declared bus segregation laws unconstitutional.

In the evening two simultaneous mass meetings emphasized love, dignity, and refusal to ride on the buses until segregation was abolished. That night the Ku Klux Klan rode through the Negro district. Instead of dark, locked houses of terrified Negroes, the K.K.K. found the lights on, the doors open and people watching the Klan parade. A few even waved. Nonplussed, the Klan disappeared.

With the car pool prohibited, each area worked out its own share-the-ride plan, and many people walked. The buses remained empty. In the mass meetings detailed plans were presented for resuming—after over a year—the use of the buses on an integrated basis. There must be courtesy. This was a victory, not over the white man, but for justice and democracy.

The Supreme Court's antisegregation order reached Montgomery on December 20. On the first day of integration, there were no major incidents. Then the white extremists began a reign of terror. Shots were fired at buses; a teen-age girl was beaten; a pregnant Negro woman was shot; the Klan paraded again and burned crosses. But the Negroes' fear had gone. The homes of more leaders and several Negro churches were bombed. This terrorism repelled many whites. The local newspaper, several white ministers, and the businessmen's association denounced the bombings.

The Negroes kept nonviolent discipline. More bombs exploded. Although arrested whites were quickly found "not guilty," the terrorism abruptly ceased. Desegregation then proceeded smoothly, a compliance virtually inconceivable a year before.

## CONTINUING DEVELOPMENT

Throughout the world there has also been other significant nonviolent action, some of which occurred before these examples and some of it since. Other important cases are likely to have occurred before this book is in print. Major strikes and nonviolent demonstrations in Franco's Spain are scarcely mentioned here, for example, and there appear to be a large number of unstudied Latin American, as well as African, cases.

In the non-Gandhian development of nonviolent action in the mid-twentieth century particular struggles were often tinged with violence. Sometimes the nonviolent action took place side by side with violence. Sometimes it occurred before or after the violence—both in the case of Hungary in 1956-57. Nevertheless, the power of these various struggles has been predominantly rooted in mass solidarity and popular nonviolent defiance. The reasons for this essentially nonviolent quality have varied. Sometimes people recognized the practical limitations of violence—for example, in 1968 Czechs and Slovaks recalled the violent phase of the 1956 Hungarian Revolution as a pattern not to be imitated. Sometimes people have felt a revulsion against cruelty and killing for political ends, having seen so much of it. For example, some East Germans in June 1953 shouted: "We want a *decent* revolution." More frequently, probably, people have simply seen methods of nonviolent action as ways to act, ways which gave them a sense of their own power and perhaps also offered a reasonable chance of success in gaining their objectives. This seems to have been the case, for example, in Norway in 1942 and in El Salvador and Guatemala in 1944.

The development of nonviolent action of various types continues throughout the world, arising from different roots, taking numerous forms in response to a multitude of situations and problems. Struggles against war, for civil liberties, for social revolution, against home-grown and foreign-imposed dictatorships, and for a determining voice in their own lives by people who feel powerless are now leading to a continuing application of nonviolent action. This type of resistance is also likely to be used by persons and groups who find the direction or speed of change distasteful. In addition, as knowledge of this technique spreads, groups who attempt to suspend constitutional government gracefully or to destroy it blatantly may find themselves confronted with unexpectedly effective resistance.

The experiments made under Gandhi's political leadership, and also his thought and activities, still sometimes stimulate or strongly influence new nonviolent struggles. But even in such cases the Gandhian component has often been modified in new cultural and political settings. Frequently, as in anti-Nazi resistance movements and in Czechoslovakia in 1968, there is no clear link between the Gandhian experiments and new cases of nonviolent struggle. As those *satyagraha* campaigns recede into history they are less and less a direct factor in these new struggles. It is always possible, however, that this might be reversed if serious new interest should develop in Gandhi as a political strategist. It must be noted, however, that whatever may be the stimuli and motivations, in the twentieth century a remarkable expansion has taken place in the use of nonviolent struggle as a substitute for violence in a widening variety of political conflicts.

Needless to say, there have been setbacks in this development. At times there has appeared a clear trend toward the abandonment of nonviolent action in favor of violence. For example, the limited and sporadic use of nonviolent action both by nonwhites in South Africa[45] and by Afro-Americans in the United States was followed in each case by advocacy of violence. Nevertheless, when seen in historical perspective there has been a relative burst of development in this technique in the twentieth century. However unevenly, the process continues. One of the evidences for this was the unprepared use for some weeks of widespread and courageous nonviolent resistance by the Czechs and Slovaks following the invasion by the Soviet Union and her allies on August 21, 1968.

## A. Czechoslovakia—1968[46]

The Soviet leaders expected that the massive invasion of Czechoslovakia by more than half a million Warsaw Treaty Organization troops would overwhelm the much smaller Czechoslovak army within days, leaving the country in confusion and defeat. The invasion would also make possible a *coup d'état* to replace the reform-minded Dubček regime with a conservative pro-Moscow one. With this in mind, the Soviet

K.G.B. (State Police) kidnapped the Communist Party's First Secretary, Alexander Dubcek; the Prime Minister, Oldrich Černik; the National Assembly President, Josef Smrkovsky; and the National Front Chairman, František Kriegel. The Soviet officials held under house arrest the President of the Republic, Ludvik Svoboda, who was a popular soldier-statesman in both Czechoslovakia and the Soviet Union. They hoped that he would give the mantle of legitimacy to the new conservative regime. The kidnapped leaders might have been killed once the *coup* had been successful, as happened in Hungary in 1957.

But the country was not demoralized as a result of military defeat, for it was a different type of resistance which was waged. Nor did a puppet regime quickly replace the kidnapped leaders. The Czechoslovak officials sent emergency orders to all the armed forces to remain in their barracks. The Soviet leaders had expected that the situation would be so effectively under control within three days that the invading troops could be then withdrawn. This did not happen, and as a result there were serious logistical and morale problems among the invading troops. Owing to resistance at several strategic points a collaborationist government was prevented, at least for about eight months—until April 1969 when the Husak regime came in.

Resistance began in early hours of the invasion. Employees of the government news agency (Č.T.K.) refused orders to issue a release stating that certain Czechoslovak party and governmental officials had requested the invasion. Also, President Svoboda courageously refused to sign the document presented to him by the conservative clique. Finally, it was possible through the clandestine radio network to convene several official bodies, and these opposed the invasion.

The Extraordinary Fourteenth Party Congress, the National Assembly, and what was left of the government ministers all issued statements similar to the emergency statement by the Party Presidium before the arrival of the K.G.B.—that the invasion had begun without the knowledge of party or governmental leaders; there had been no "request." Some of the bodies selected interim leaders who carried out certain emergency functions. The National Assembly went on to "demand the release from detention of our constitutional representatives . . . in order that they can carry out their constitutional functions entrusted to them by the Sovereign people of the country," and to "demand immediate withdrawal of the armies of the five states."[47]

The clandestine radio network during the first week both created many forms of resistance and shaped others: it convened the Extraordinary Fourteenth Party Congress, called one-hour general strikes, requested the rail workers to slow the transport of Russian tracking and jamming equipment, and discouraged collaboration within the Č.S.S.R. State Police. There is no record of any collaboration among the uniformed Public Police; indeed, many of them worked actively with the resistance. The radio argued the futility of acts of violence and the wisdom of nonviolent resistance. It instructed students in the streets to clear out of potentially explosive situations and cautioned against rumors. The radio was the main means through which a politically mature and effective resistance was shaped. Colin Chapman has observed that "each form of resistance, however ineffective it might have been alone, served to strengthen the other manifestations,"[48] and through the radio different levels of resistance and different parts of the country were kept in steady communication. With many government agencies put out of operation by Russian occupation of their offices, the radio also took on certain emergency functions (such as obtaining manpower to bring in potato and hops harvests) and provided vital information. This ranged from assuring mothers that their children in summer camps were safe to reporting meager news of the Moscow negotiations.

Militarily totally successful, the Russians now faced a strong political struggle. In face of unified civilian resistance, the absence of a collaborationist government, and the increasing demoralization of their troops, the Soviet leaders agreed on Friday, the 23rd, that President Svoboda would fly to Moscow for negotiations. Svoboda refused to negotiate until Dubček, Cernik, and Smrkovsky joined the discussions. In four days a compromise was worked out. This left most of the leaders in their positions but called for the party to exercise more fully its "leading role," and left Russian troops in the country. The compromise seems also to have included the sacrifice of certain reform-minded leaders and reforms.

That first week the entire people had in a thousand ways courageously and cleverly fought an exhilarating battle for their freedom. The compromise, called the Moscow Protocol, created severely mixed feelings among the people. Observers abroad saw this as an unexpected success for the nation and its leaders; an occupied country is not supposed to have bargaining power. But most Czechs and Slovaks saw it as a defeat and for a week would not accept it. The leaders were apparently doubtful of the disciplined capacity of the populace for sustained resistance in the face of severe repression.

Despite the absence of prior planning or explicit training for civilian resistance, the Dubček regime managed to remain in power until April

1969, about eight months longer than would have been possible with military resistance. The Russians subsequently gained important objectives, including the establishment of a conservative regime. The final outcome of the struggle and occupation remains undetermined at this writing. Nevertheless, this highly significant case requires careful research and analysis of its methods, problems, successes and failures.

## SEEKING INSIGHT

This brief sketch of the historical development of nonviolent action does not convey the extent and significance of the past use of this technique. Nevertheless, even this survey and the various illustrative cases cited throughout the remainder of this book are sufficient to call into question and even to refute some of the main misconceptions which have been widely accepted concerning this type of action.

Extensive use of nonviolent action has occurred despite the absence of attention to the development of the technique itself. Its practice has been partly spontaneous, partly intuitive, partly vaguely patterned after some known case. It has usually been practiced under highly unfavorable conditions and with a lack of experienced participants or even experienced leaders. Almost always there were no advance preparations or training, little or no planning or prior consideration of strategy and tactics and of the range of methods. The people using it have usually had little real understanding of the nature of the technique which they sought to wield and were largely ignorant of its history. There were no studies of strategy and tactics for them to consult, or handbooks on how to organize the "troops," conduct the struggle, and maintain discipline. Under such conditions it is not surprising that there have often been defeats or only partial victories, or that violence has sometimes erupted—which, as we shall see, helps to bring defeat. With such handicaps, it is amazing that the practice of the technique has been as widespread, successful and orderly as it has.

Some men and women are now trying to learn more of the nature of this technique and to explore its potentialities. Some people are now asking how nonviolent action can be refined and applied in place of violence to meet complex and difficult problems. These intellectual efforts are a potentially significant new factor in the history of this technique. It remains to be seen what consequences this factor may have for the future development of nonviolent action.

# NOTES

1. For a fuller discussion of this theory of controlling the power of rulers, see Chapter One.

2. See, for example, Bart. de Ligt, **The Conquest of Violence: An Essay on War and Revolution** (New York: E. P. Dutton & Co., 1938, and London: George Routledge & Sons, 1937), pp. 26-27; Richard Gregg, **The Power of Nonviolence** (Second rev. ed.; New York: Schocken Books, Schocken Paperback, 1966, and London: James Clarke & Co., 1960), pp. 93-94 and 98-100; Krishnalal Shridharani, **War Without Violence: A Study of Gandhi's Method and Its Accomplishments** (New York: Harcourt Brace & Co., 1939, and London: Victor Gollancz, 1939), U.S. ed., pp. 276-294; Br. ed., pp. 237-246; and T. K. Mahadevan, Adam Roberts and Gene Sharp, eds., **Civilian Defence: An Introduction** (New Delhi: Gandhi Peace Foundation and Bombay: Bharatiya Vidya Bhavan, 1967) Appendices Four and Five (consisting of quotations on the point from R. R. Diwakar, N. K. Bose, K. Shridharani, and R. Gregg), pp. 249-254.

3. This is a revision of the definition first published in Gene Sharp, "The Meanings of Nonviolence: A Typology (revised)," **Journal of Conflict Resolution**, vol. III, no. 1 (March 1959), pp. 44-45. The definition is largely compatible with, although not based upon, that offered by Niels Lindberg, *"Indledning og Problemstilling,"* in Karl Ehrlich (pseud. of Karl Raloff), Niels Lindberg and Gammelgaard Jacobson, **Kamp Uden Vaaben: Ikke-Vold som Kampmiddel mod Krig og Undertrykkelse** (Copenhagen: Levin & Munksgaard, Ejnar Munksgaard, 1937), pp. 9-13.

4. See Gene Sharp, "The Origins of Gandhi's Nonviolent Militancy" (review-essay on **Gandhi's Truth** by Erik Erikson). **Harvard Political Review**, vol. II, no. 1 (May 1970), pp. 13-14 and 34-39.

5. F. R. Cowell, **The Revolutions of Ancient Rome** (New York: Frederick A. Praeger, 1962, and London: Thames and Hudson, 1962), pp. 42-43. Cowell's account is based on Livy.

6. Theodor Mommsen, **The History of Rome**, trans. William Purdie Dickson, rev. ed. (London: Richard Bentley & Son, 1894), vol. I, pp. 346-350. An excerpt appears in Mulford Q. Sibley, ed., **The Quiet Battle: Writings on the Theory and Practice of Non-violent Resistance** (Garden City, N.Y.: Doubleday, Anchor Books, 1963), pp. 108-110.

7. Daniel Dulany, **Considerations upon the Rights of the Colonists to the Privileges of British Subjects** (New York, 1766), p. 47, quoted in Edmund S. and Helen M. Morgan, **The Stamp Act Crisis: Prologue to Revolution** (Rev. ed.; New York: Collier Books, 1963), p. 118.

8. See esp. Morgan and Morgan, **The Stamp Act Crisis**; Arthur M. Schlesinger, **The Colonial Merchants and the American Revolution, 1763-1776** (New York: Frederick Ungar, 1966); and Lawrence Henry Gipson, **The British Empire Before the American Revolution**, vol. X, **The Triumphant Empire: Thunderclouds Gather in the West, 1763-1766**, vol. XI, **The Triumphant Empire: The**

Rumbling of the Coming Storm, 1766-1770, and vol. XII, The Triumphant Empire: Britain Sails into the Storm, 1770-1776 (New York: Alfred A. Knopf, 1961-1965).

9. See Leo Tolstoy, The Kingdom of God is Within You, and "A Letter to A Hindu."

10. See Henry David Thoreau, On the Duty of Civil Disobedience (pamphlet; Introduction by Gene Sharp; London: Peace News, 1963).

11. *Ibid.*, pp. 11 and 13.

12. On the 1905 Revolution, see Sidney Harcave, First Blood: The Russian Revolution of 1905 (New York: Macmillan, 1964, and London: Collier-Macmillan, 1964); Solomon M. Schwarz, The Russian Revolution of 1905: The Workers' Movement and the Formation of Bolshevism and Menshevism. Trans. by Gertrude Vakar, with a Preface by Leopold H. Haimson (Chicago and London: University of Chicago Press, 1967), esp. pp. 129-195. Also see Richard Charques, The Twilight of Imperial Russia (London: Phoenix House, 1958), pp. 111-139: Leonard Schapiro, The Communist Party of the Soviet Union (New York: Random House, 1960, and London: Eyre & Spottiswoode, 1960), pp. 63-70 and 75; Hugh Seton-Watson, The Decline of Imperial Russia, 1855-1914 (New York: Frederick A. Praeger and London: Methuen & Co., 1952), pp. 219-260; Bertram D. Wolfe, Three Who Made a Revolution (New York: Dial Press, 1948, and London: Thames and Hudson, 1956), pp. 278-336; and Michael Prawdin, The Unmentionable Nechaev: A Key to Bolshevism (London: Allen and Unwin, 1961), pp. 147-149.

13. See Wilfred Harris Crook, The General Strike, pp. 496-527; Goodspeed, The Conspirators, pp. 108-143 and 211-213; Halperin, Germany Tried Democracy, pp. 168-188; Eyck, A History of the Weimar Republic, vol. I, pp. 129-160; Karl Raloff (pseud.: Karl Ehrlich), *"Den Ikkevoldelige Modstand, der Kvalte Kapp-Kupet,* in Ehrlich, Lindberg and Jacobson, Kamp Uden Vaaben, pp. 194-213; and Wheeler-Bennett, The Nemesis of Power, pp. 63-82.

14. Crook, The General Strike, p. 513.

15. Goodspeed, The Conspirators, pp. 211-213.

16. Eyck, A History of the Weimar Republic, vol. I, p. 154.

17. On the *Ruhrkampf,* see Wolfgang Sternstein, "The *Ruhrkampf* of 1923: Economic Problems of Civilian Defence," in Adam Roberts, ed., Civilian Resistance as a National Defense: Nonviolent Action Against Aggression (Harrisburg, Pa.: Stackpole Books, 1968); British edition: The Strategy of Civilian Defence: Nonviolent Resistance to Aggression (London: Faber and Faber, 1967), pp. 106-135. (Note: the paperback edition is entitled Civilian Resistance as a National Defense [Baltimore, Md. and Harmondsworth, Middlesex, England: Penguin Books, 1969] but all page references cited in notes in this volume refer to the hardbook editions.) See also Karl Raloff (psud.: Karl Ehrlich), "Ruhrkampen," in Ehrlich, Lindberg and Jacobsen, Kamp Uden Vaaben, pp. 181-193; Wheeler-Bennett, The Nemesis of Power, pp. 102-109; Halperin, Germany Tried Democracy, pp. 246-260 and pp. 288-289; and Eyck, A History of The Weimar Republic, vol. I, pp. 232-306 *passim.*

18. This account was originally published in Gene Sharp, "Creative Conflict in Politics," The New Era, January 1962; pamphlet reprint ed., p. 4 (London: Housmans, 1962). See Joan V. Bondurant, Conquest of Violence: The Gandhian Philosophy of Conflict (Princeton, N.J.: Princeton University Press, 1958), pp. 46-52; Gandhi, Non-violent Resistance; Ind. ed.: Satyagraha, pp. 177-203; and Mahadev Desai, The Epic of Travancore (Ahmedabad: Navajivan, 1937).

19. M. K. Gandhi, Indian Opinion, Golden Number, 1914; quoted in Gandhi, Non-violent Resistance, p. 35; Ind. ed.: Satyagraha, p. 35.

20. M. K. Gandhi, Hind Swaraj or Indian Home Rule, p. 100.

21. Quoted in Sharp, Gandhi Wields the Weapon of Moral Power, p. 54.

22. Gandhi, Young India, 29 September 1921; quoted in Clarence Marsh Case, Non-violent Coercion, p. 392.

23. Gandhi, Young India, 4 August 1920; quoted in Gandhi, Non-violent Resistance p. 127; Ind. ed., Satyagraha, p. 127.

24. Gandhi, Young India, 27 March 1930; quoted in Sharp, Gandhi Wields . . . , p. 82.

25. All-India Congress Committee, Congress Bulletin, 7 March 1930, no. 5; quoted in Sharp, Gandhi Wields . . . , p. 64. For a brief discussion of some popular misconceptions about Gandhi and his activities, see Gene Sharp, "Gandhi's Political Significance Today," in G. Ramachandran and T. K. Mahadevan, eds., Gandhi: His Relevance for Our Times (Berkeley, Calif.: World Without War Council, 1971, and New Delhi: Gandhi Peace Foundation, and Bombay: Bharatiya Vidya Bhavan, 1967), pp. 137-157.

26. Ranganath R. Diwaker, Satyagraha: Its Technique and History (Bombay: Hind Kitabs, 1946), p. 55.

27. This account was also originally published in "Creative Conflict in Politics." See Sharp, Gandhi Wields The Weapon of Moral Power, pp. 37-226, and S. Gopal The Viceroyalty of Lord Irwin, 1926-1931 (London: Oxford University Press, 1957), pp. 54-122.

28. Jawaharlal Nehru, Toward Freedom, p. 80.

29. See for example, Warmbrunn, The Dutch Under German Occupation 1940-1945. Further references are cited.

30. See, for example, Magne Skodvin, "Norwegian Nonviolent Resistance During the German Occupation," in Roberts, ed., Civilian Resistance as a National Defense, pp. 136-153; Br. ed.: The Strategy of Civilian Defence, pp. 136-153. Further references are cited.

31. See for example, Jeremy Bennett, "The Resistance Against the German Occupation of Denmark 1940-5," in Roberts, ed., Civilian Resistance as a National Defense pp. 154-172; Br. ed.: The Strategy of Civilian Defence, pp. 154-172. Further references are cited.

32. This sketch also was originally published in "Creative Conflict in Politics." See Sharp, Tyranny Could Not Quell Them (pamphlet) (London: Peace News, 1958 and later editions). Norwegian sources include: Magnus Jensen, "Kampen om Skolen," in Sverre Steen, general editor, Norges Krig (Oslo: Gyldendal Norsk Forlag, 1947-50), vol. III, pp. 73-105, and Sverre S. Amundsen, gen. ed., Kirkenes Ferda, 1942 (Oslo: J. W. Cappelens Forlag, 1946).

33. From Heinz Ullstein's memoirs Spielplatz meines Lebens (Munich: Kindler Verlag, 1961), pp. 338-340. This passage (translated by Hilda Morris) is reprinted from Theodor Ebert, "Effects of Repression by the Invader," Peace News, 19 March 1965.

34. This account is based upon Mario Rosenthal, Guatemala: The Story of an Emergent Latin-American Democracy (New York: Twayne Publishers, 1962) pp. 191-214, and Ronald M. Schneider, Communism in Guatemala 1944-1954 (New York: Frederick A. Praeger, 1958), pp. 5-14.

35. Rosenthal, Guatemala, p. 201.

36. Ibid., p. 210.

37. *Ibid.,* p. 211.

38. *Ibid.,* p. 200.

39. *Ibid.,* pp. 201-202.

40. See, for example, Theodor Ebert, "Nonviolent Resistance Against Communist Regimes?" in Roberts, ed., **Civilian Resistance as a National Defense,** pp. 175-194; Br. ed.: **The Strategy of Civilian Defence,** pp. 175-194. Further references are cited.

41. See, for example, **Report of the Special Committee on the Problem of Hungary** (New York: United Nations, General Assembly Official Records, Eleventh Session, Supplement No. 18-A/3592, 1957).

42. This sketch also was originally published in "Creative Conflict in Politics." See Brigitte Gerland, "How the Great Vorkuta Strike was Prepared," and "The Great Labor Camp Strike at Vorkuta," in the weekly *The Militant* (New York), 28 February and 7 March 1955, and Joseph Scholmer, "Vorkuta: Strike in a Concentration Camp," in Sibley, ed., **The Quiet Battle,** pp. 187-204, reprinted from Scholmer, *Vorkuta* (New York: Henry Holt & Co., 1955).

43. **Monthly Information Bulletin of the International Commission Against Concentration Camp Practices** (Brussels), no. 4 (August-November 1955); See especially Paul Barton's article "The Strike Mechanism in Soviet Concentration Camps."

44. This sketch was originally published in Sharp, "Creative Conflict in Politics." See, for example, Martin Luther King, Jr., **Stride Toward Freedom: The Montgomery Story** (New York: Ballantine Books, 1958, and London: Victor Gollancz, 1959).

45. For a discussion of strategic problems of resistance in South Africa, and the potentialities of nonviolent action there, see Sharp, "Can Non-Violence Work in South Africa?", "Problems of Violent and Non-Violent Struggle," "Strategic Problems of the South African Resistance," and "How Do You Get Rid of Oppression?", in the weekly *Peace News* (London) 21 June, 28 June, 5 July, and 25 October 1963.

46. This account is based on a draft prepared by Carl Horne. The following sources may be consulted for further details of this case: Robert Littell, ed., **The Czech Black Book** (New York: Frederick A. Praeger, 1969); Robin Alison Remington, ed., **Winter in Prague** (Cambridge, Mass.:M.I.T. Press,1969); Joseph Wechsberg, **The Voices** (Garden City, N.Y.: Doubleday, 1969); and Philip Windsor and Adam Roberts, **Czechoslovakia 1968** (New York: Columbia University Press, 1969 and London: Chatto & Windus, 1969).

47. Remington, ed., **Winter in Prague,** p. 382.

48. Colin Chapman, **August 21st** (Philadelphia: Lippincott, 1968), p. 44.

# Acknowledgments

Appreciation is gratefully acknowledged to the authors and publishers whose works are quoted in this volume. Complete publication details are provided in the footnotes and bibliography.

Aptheker, Herbert, *American Negro Slave Revolts.* Copyright © 1963 by International Publishers, Inc. New York: International Publishers, 1964. Permission courtesy of International Publishers, Inc.

Bailey, Thomas A., *A Diplomatic History of the American People.* Sixth edition. Copyrighted. New York: Appleton-Century-Crofts, 1958. Permission courtesy of Appleton-Century-Crofts.

Bauer, Raymond A. and Alice H. Bauer, "Day to Day Resistance to Slavery," *Journal of Negro History*, vol. XXVII, no. 4 (Oct. 1942), pp. 388-419. Copyright © 1942 by the Association for the Study of African-American Life and History, Inc. Permission courtesy The Association for the Study of African-American Life and History, Inc., and Raymond A. and Alice H. Bauer.

Blum, Robert, *The United States and China in World Affairs.* ed. by A. Doak Barnett. Copyright © 1966 by the Council on Foreign Relations. New York: McGraw-Hill (for the Council on Foreign Relations), 1966. Permission courtesy McGraw-Hill Book Co.

Bondurant, Joan V., *Conquest of Violence: The Gandhian Philosophy of*

*Conflict.* Copyright © 1958 by Princeton University Press. Princeton, New Jersey: Princeton University Press. London: Oxford University Press, 1958. Passages reprinted by permission of Princeton University Press.

Borton, Hugh, *Peasant Uprisings in Japan of the Tokugawa Period.* Second Edition. New York: Paragon Book Reprint Corp., 1968. First published in *The Transactions of the Asiatic Society of Japan* (Second Series), vol. XVI, 1939. Passage reprinted courtesy of Paragon Book Reprint Corp.

Brant, Stefan, *The East German Rising.* Translated and adapted by Charles Wheeler. Copyright © 1955 by Stefan Brant. New York: Frederick A. Praeger, 1957. London: Thames and Hudson, 1955. Permission courtesy of Praeger Publishers, Inc.

Brinton, Crane, *The Anatomy of Revolution.* Copyright © Prentice-Hall Inc. Englewood Cliffs, N.J. New York: Vintage Books, 1962. Passages reprinted with permission of Prentice-Hall, Inc.

Case, Clarence Marsh, *Nonviolent Coercion: A Study in Methods of Social Pressure.* Copyright 1923. New York: The Century Co., 1923. Permission courtesy of Appleton-Century-Crofts, Inc.

Charques, Richard, *Twilight of Imperial Russia.* Copyright © 1958 by Richard Charques. Fair Lawn, N. J.: Essential Books, 1959. London: Phoenix House, 1958. Permission courtesy of Dorothy Charques.

Clark, Evans, ed., *Boycotts and Peace.* New York and London: Harper & Bros., 1932. Permission courtesy Harper & Row Publishers, Inc.

Crankshaw, Edward, *Gestapo: Instrument of Tyranny.* Copyright 1956. New York: Viking Press, 1956. London: Putnam, 1956. Permission courtesy of Edward Crankshaw.

Crook, Wilfrid H., *The General Strike: A Study of Labor's Tragic Weapon in Theory and Practice.* Chapel Hill: University of North Carolina Press, 1931. Passages reprinted by permission of the Shoe String Press, Inc., present copyright owner.

Dallin, Alexander, *German Rule in Russia, 1941-1945: A Study of Occupation Policies.* Copyright 1957. New York: St. Martin's Press, 1957. London: Macmillan, 1957. Permission courtesy of St. Martin's Press and Macmillan, London and Basingstoke.

Daniels, Jonathan, *Frontiers on the Potomac.* New York: Macmillan, 1946. Permission courtesy of Brandt & Brandt.

Davison, W. Phillips, *The Berlin Blockade: A Study in Cold War Politics.* Copyright © 1958 by the Rand Corporation. Princeton, N. J.: Princeton University Press, 1958. Passage reprinted by permission of Princeton University Press.

Deanesly, Margaret, *A History of the Medieval Church, 590-1500.* London: Methuen & Co., 1965. Permission courtesy of Associated Book Publishers Ltd.

Delarue, Jacques, *The Gestapo: A History of Horror.* New York: William Morrow, 1964. Passages reprinted courtesy of Macdonald & Co. (Publishers) Ltd.

Ebert, Theodor, "Theory and Practice of Nonviolent Resistance," unpublished English translation of a doctoral thesis presented at the University of Erlangen, Germany, 1965. Permission courtesy of Theodor Ebert.

Eyck, Erich, *A History of the Weimar Republic,* Vol. I. *From the Collapse of the Empire to Hindenburg's Election.* Copyright © 1962 by the President and Fellows of Harvard College. Cambridge, Mass.: Harvard University Press, 1962. Permission courtesy of Harvard University Press.

Farmer, James, *Freedom—When?* Copyright © 1965 by the Congress of Racial Equality, Inc. New York: Random House, 1965. Permission courtesy of James Farmer and Random House.

Faulkner, William, *A Fable.* Copyright © 1950, 1954 by William Faulkner. New York: Random House, 1954. Permission courtesy of Random House, Inc.

Fogg, Richard W., "Jazz Under the Nazis," in *Music 66, "down beat*'s Annual," 1966, pp. 97-99. Copyright © 1966 by *down beat*, 1966. Permission courtesy of *down beat.*

Frank, Jerome D., *Sanity and Survival: Psychological Aspects of War and Peace.* Copyright © 1967 by Jerome D. Frank. New York: Random House and Vintage Books, 1968. Permission courtesy of Jerome D. Frank.

Friedrich, Carl J., ed., *Totalitarianism.* Copyright © 1954 by President and Fellows of Harvard College. Cambridge, Mass.: Harvard University Press, 1954. Permission courtesy of Harvard University Press.

Gandhi, M. K., *An Autobiography, The Constructive Programme, Economics of Khadi, Hind Swaraj, Non-violence in Peace and War,* Two vols., *Satyagraha, Satyagraha in South Africa, Young India,* Vol. I; publication details as cited in the bibliography; Gandhi's works are copyrighted by Navajivan Trust, Ahmedabad, India, and the passages reproduced in this volume are reprinted with the permission and courtesy of Navajivan Trust.

Gipson, Lawrence Henry, *The British Empire Before the American Revolution,* vols. X, XI and XII (see Bibliography). Copyright © by Alfred A. Knopf, 1961, 1965 and 1965 respectively. New York: Alfred A. Knopf, 1961-1965. Permission courtesy of Alfred A. Knopf, Inc.

——, *The Coming of the Revolution, 1763-1775.* Copyright © 1954 by Harper and Brothers. New York and Evanston: Harper Torchbooks, 1962. Permission courtesy of Harper & Row, Publishers, Inc.

Goodspeed, D. J., *The Conspirators: A Study of the Coup d'Etat.* Copyright © 1962 by D. J. Goodspeed, 1962. New York: Viking Press, 1962. Toronto: Macmillan Co. of Canada, 1962. Permission courtesy of Viking Press and of Macmillan (London and Basingstoke).

Gopal, S., *The Viceroyalty of Lord Irwin, 1926-1931.* Copyright 1957. London: Oxford University Press, 1957. Permission courtesy of Oxford University Press.

Görlitz, Walter, ed., *The Memoirs of Field-Marshal Keitel.* Trans. by David Irving. Copyright © 1965 by William Kimber and Co., Ltd. Passages reprinted with permission of William Kimber and Co., Ltd., and Stein and Day Publishers.

Gregg, Richard B., *The Power of Nonviolence.* Second revised edition. Copyright © 1935, 1959, 1966 by Richard B. Gregg. New York: Schocken, 1966. London: James Clarke & Co., 1960. Permission courtesy Schocken Books Inc. for Richard B. Gregg.

Halberstam, David, *The Making of a Quagmire.* Copyright © 1964, 1965 by David Halberstam. New York: Random House, 1965. London: The Bodley Head, 1965. Permission courtesy of Random House.

Halperin, S. William, *Germany Tried Democracy: A Political History of the*

Press and Oxford University Press.

Kuper, Leo, *Passive Resistance in South Africa*. New Haven, Conn.: Yale University Press, 1957. London: Jonathan Cape, 1956. Permission courtesy of Yale University Press and Leo Kuper.

Lasswell, Harold D., *Power and Personality*. Copyright © 1948 by W. W. Norton & Co., Inc. New York: W. W. Norton & Co., 1948. Permission courtesy W. W. Norton & Co., Inc.

Lenin, V. I., *Selected Works in Three Volumes*. English language translations copyrighted. New York: International Publishers, and Moscow: Progress Publishers, 1967. Passages reprinted with permission of International Publishers, Inc.

Liddell Hart, Sir Basil, *Strategy: The Indirect Approach*. Coprighted. New York: Frederick A. Praeger, 1954. London: Faber & Faber, 1954. Permission courtesy of Lady Kathleen Liddell Hart.

Littell, Robert, ed., *The Czech Black Book: Prepared by the Institute of History of the Czechoslovak Academy of Sciences*. Copyright © 1969 by Praeger Publishers, Inc., New York. New York, Washington and London: Frederick A. Praeger, 1969.

Lochner, Louis P., ed., *The Goebbels Diaries, 1942-1943*. Copyright © 1948 by the Fireside Press, Inc. Garden City, New York: Doubleday & Co., 1948. Permission courtesy of Doubleday & Co., Inc.

Loh, Robert (as told to Humphrey Evans), *Escape from Red China*. Copyright © 1962 by Robert Loh and Humphrey Evans. New York: Coward-McCann, 1962. Passages reprinted by permission of Coward, McCann and Geoghegan, Inc.

Luthuli, Albert, *Let My People Go: An Autobiography*. Copyright © 1962 by Albert Luthuli. New York: McGraw-Hill Book Co., Inc., 1962. London: Collins, 1962. Used with permission of McGraw-Hill Book Co., Inc.

Mabee, Carleton, *Black Freedom: The Nonviolent Abolitionists from 1830 Through the Civil War*. Copyright © 1970 by Carleton Mabee. New York: Macmillan, 1970. Toronto: Macmillan, 1970. London: Collier-Macmillan, 1970. Permission courtesy of The Macmillan Co.

MacIver, R. M., *The Web of Government*. Copyright © 1947, 1965 by Robert MacIver. New York: Macmillan, 1947.

Miller, William Robert, *Nonviolence: A Christian Interpretation*. Copyright © 1964 by National Board of Young Men's Christian Association. New York: Association Press, 1964. Permission courtesy of Association Press.

Morgan, Edmund S. and Helen M., *The Stamp Act Crisis: Prologue to Revolution*. New, revised edition. Copyright © 1953 by the University of North Carolina Press; Copyright © 1962 by Edmund S. Morgan. New York: Collier Books, 1963. Permission courtesy of Edmund S. Morgan, the University of North Carolina Press and the Institute of Early American History and Culture, Williamsburg.

Mosca, Gaetano, *The Ruling Class*. Introduction by Arthur Livingstone. Copyright © 1939 by McGraw-Hill. New York and London: McGraw-Hill, 1939. Permission courtesy McGraw-Hill Book Co.

Jawaharlal Nehru, *An Autobiography* (sometimes cited as *Jawaharlal Nehru: An Autobiography*). New edition. London: The Bodley Head, 1953. Excerpts quoted with permission of The Bodley Head and the John Day Company. U.S. copyright: Copyright © 1941, The John Day Company.

Renewed 1968 by Indira Gandhi.

——, *Toward Freedom: The Autobiography of Jawaharlal Nehru.* Revised edition. Copyright 1941, The John Day Company, New York: John Day Co., 1942. Permission courtesy of The John Day Co., Ind., publishers.

Neumann, Franz, *Behemoth: The Structure and Practice of National Socialism, 1933-1944.* Copyright © 1942, 1944 by Oxford University Press, New York. New York: Octagon Books, 1963. Passages reprinted courtesy of Farrar, Straus & Giroux, Inc.

Neustadt, Richard E., *Presidential Power: The Politics of Leadership.* Copyright © 1960, 1964 by John Wiley & Sons, Inc. New York and London: John Wiley and Sons, 1960. Permission courtesy John Wiley & Sons, Inc.

Nicholson, Harold, *Diplomacy.* Second edition. Copyrighted 1950, 1960. London, New York and Toronto: Oxford University Press, 1960 [1950]. Permission courtesy of Oxford University Press.

Nickalls, John L., ed., *The Journals of George Fox.* Cambridge: University Press, 1952. Quotations reprinted by permission of Cambridge University Press.

Oppenheimer, Martin and George Lakey, *A Manual for Direct Action.* Copyright © 1964, 1965 by Martin Oppenheimer, George Lakey, and the Friends Peace Committee. Chicago: Quadrangle Books, 1965. Permission courtesy of Quadrangle Books.

*Peace News* (London), passage from issue of July 2, 1965. Permission courtesy of Peace News Ltd.

Peck, Graham, *Two Kinds of Time.* Copyright © 1950 by Graham Peck. Houghton Mifflin, 1950. Permission courtesy of Houghton Mifflin Co.

Peck, James, *Freedom Ride.* Copyright © 1962 by James Peck. New York: Simon & Schuster, 1962. Permission courtesy Simon & Schuster.

**The Pentagon Papers as published by "The New York Times",** Copyright © 1971 by The New York Times Company. New York, Toronto and London: Bantam Books, 1971. Permission courtesy of *The New York Times.*

Prawdin, Michael, **The Unmentionable Nechaev: A Key to Bolshevism.** Copyright 1961. London: Allen and Unwin, 1961. Permission courtesy of Reneé C. Prawdin.

Rayback, Joseph G., *A History of American Labor.* Copyright © 1959, 1965 by Joseph G. Rayback. New York, Macmillan, 1964. Permission courtesy of The Macmillan Co.

Révész, Imre, *History of the Hungarian Reformed Church.* Washington, D.C.: Hungarian Reformed Federation of America, 1956. Passage reprinted from p. 128. Courtesy of the Hungarian Reformed Federation of America.

Reynolds, Lloyd G., *Labor Economics and Labor Relations.* Copyright © 1949 by Prentice-Hall, Inc. Englewood Cliffs, New Jersey: Prentice-Hall, 1959. Permission courtesy of Prentice-Hall, Inc.

Roberts, Adam, "Buddhism and Politics in South Vietnam," in *The World Today* (London), vol. 21, no. 6 (June 1965), pp. 240-250. Permission courtesy of Adam Roberts.

——, *Civilian Resistance as a National Defence.* Harrisburg, Pa., Stackpole Books, 1968. Original British edition: *The Strategy of Civilian Defence.* Copyright © 1967 by Adam Roberts, 1967. London: Faber & Faber, 1967. Permission courtesy of Adam Roberts.

Rosenthal, Mario, *Guatemala: The Story of an Emergent Latin American Democracy.* Copyrighted, New York: Twayne Publishers, 1962. Permission courtesy of Twayne Publishers, Inc.

Rostovtzeff, M., *The Social and Economic History of the Roman Empire*, Vol. I. Second edition revised by P. M. Frazer. Copyright © 1957 by Oxford Universtiy Press. Oxford: Clarendon Press, 1956. Permission courtesy of Clarendon Press.

Rubin, Jerry, *Do It!* New York: Simon and Schuster, 1970. Permission courtesy of Jerry Rubin.

Schapiro, Leonard, *The Communist Party of the Soviet Union.* Copyright © 1960, 1971 by Leonard Schapiro. New York: Random House, 1960. London: Eyre & Spottiswoode, 1960. Permission courtesy of Leonard B. Schapiro.

Schelling, Thomas C., *International Economics.* Copyright © 1958 by Allyn and Bacon, Inc. Boston: Allyn and Bacon, 1958.

Seifert, Harvey, *Conquest by Suffering: The Process and Prospects of Nonviolent Resistance.* Copyright © 1965 by W. L. Jenkins. Philadelphia: Westminster Press, 1965. Permission courtesy of the Westminster Press.

Seton-Watson, Christopher, *Italy From Liberalism to Fascism, 1870-1925.* Copyright © 1967 by Christopher Seton-Watson. New York: Barnes and Noble, 1967. London: Methuen, 1967. Permission courtesy of Christopher Seton-Watson.

Shirer, William L., *The Rise and Fall of the Third Reich.* Copyright © 1959, 1960 by William L. Shirer. New York: Simon and Schuster, 1960. London: Secker and Warburg, 1962. Permission courtesy of Simon and Schuster.

Shridharani, Krishnalal, *War Without Violence: A Study of Gandhi's Method and Its Accomplishments.* New York: Harcourt Brace and Co., 1939. London: Victor Gollancz, 1939. Permission courtesy of S. K. Shridharani.

Soloman, Frederic and Jacob R. Fishman, "The Psychosocial Meaning of Nonviolence in Student Civil Rights Activities", *Psychiatry,* vol. XXVII, No. 2 (May 1964), pp. 91-99. Permission courtesy of *Psychiatry: A Publication.*

Steiner, Stan, *The New Indians.* Copyright © 1968 by Stan Steiner, 1968. New York: Harper & Row, 1968. Permission courtesy of Stan Steiner and Harper & Row.

Suhl, Yuri, *They Fought Back: The Story of Jewish Resistance in Nazi Europe.* New York: Crown Publishers, 1967. London: MacGibbon and Kee, 1968. Permission courtesy of Yuri Suhl.

*Sunday Times* (London), a passage from the issue of March 19, 1967. Permission courtesy of the *Sunday Times.*

Symons, Julian, *The General Strike: A Historical Portrait.* Copyright © 1957 by Julian Symons. London: The Cresset Press. 1957. Permission courtesy of the Cresset Press, and Julian Symons.

Tabor, Robert, *M-26: Biography of a Revolution.* Copyrighted 1961. New York: Lyle Stuart, 1961. Permission courtesy of Lyle Stuart, Inc.

Taylor, George R., *The Struggle for North China.* Copyright © 1940 by the Secretariat, Institute of Pacific Relations. New York: Institute of Pacific Relations, 1940. Permission courtesy of William L. Holland, Editor, *Pacific Affairs.*

Ullstein, Heinz, *Spielplatz meines Lebens: Erinnerungen.* Copyright © 1961 by Kindler Verlag München. Munich: Kindler Verlag, 1961. Permission courtesy of Kindler Verlag. English translation in text by Hilda von

Klenze Morris.

Vassilyev, A. T., *The Ochrana: The Russian Secret Police.* Edited and with an Introduction by Rene Fülöp-Miller. Copyright © 1930 by J. B. Lippincott Co. Philadelphia and London: J. B. Lippincott Co., 1930. Passage reprinted by permission of J. B. Lippincott Company.

Warmbrunn, Werner, *The Dutch under German Occupation 1940-1945.* Copyright © 1963 by Board of Trustees of the Leland Standford Junior University. Stanford, California: Stanford University Press, 1963. London: Oxford University Press, 1963. Passages reprinted with permission of Stanford University Press.

Warriner, Doreen, *Land Reform in Principle and Practice.* Copyright © 1969 by Oxford University Press. Oxford: Clarendon Press, 1969. Permission courtesy of Clarendon Press.

Waskow, Arthur I., *From Race Riot to Sit-in: 1919 and the 1960s.* Copyright © 1966 by Doubleday and Co., Inc. Garden City, N. Y.: Doubleday, 1966. Permission courtesy of Doubleday & Co.

Wheeler-Bennett, Sir John W., *The Nemesis of Power: The Germany Army in Politics, 1918-1945.* New York: St. Martin's Press, 1953. London: Macmillan, 1953. Permission courtesy of Sir John Wheeler-Bennett.

Williams, Robin M., *The Reduction of Intergroup Tensions.* New York: Social Science Research Council, 1947. Permission courtesy of Robin M. Williams.

Wolfe, Bertram D., *Three who Made a Revolution.* Copyrighted. New York: Dial Press, 1948. London: Thames and Hudson, 1956. Permission courtesy of Bertram D. Wolfe.

Zinn, Howard, *Albany.* Atlanta: Southern Regional Council, 1962. Permission courtesy of Howard Zinn.

# recommended reading:

Thank you for purchasing this book. You may be interested in these other classic Gene Sharp books, also available from Extending Horizons Books:

### The Politics of Nonviolent Action (Three-volume set)
$25.95 (1973)

*"One of the most important books on social change and nonviolence in this century,"* —American Journal of Sociology

| | |
|---|---|
| Part 1: *Power and Struggle* | $7.95 |
| Part 2: *The Methods of Nonviolent Action* | $10.95 |
| Part 3: *The Dynamics of Nonviolent Action* | $13.95 |

### Gandhi as a Political Strategist
### With Essays on Ethics and Politics
$14.95 (1979)

A unique portrayal of this remarkable man as a shrewd, highly unorthodox political leader.

*"An in-depth analysis of Gandhi's political strategy and its relevance for social struggle today,"* — Corretta Scott King

### Social Power and Political Freedom
$8.95 paper/$15.95 cloth (1980)

A still-timely reexamination of radical politics. Includes the highly regarded essay "The Political Equivalent of War–Civilian-based Defense"

These titles, and more than 20 other modern classics, are available from booksellers or from the publisher. Catalog available upon request—

Tel: 800-342-7470 or 603-647-4383  
Fax: 603-669-7945

E-mail: orders@portersargent.com  
Web: portersargent.com

# extending horizons books

PORTER SARGENT PUBLISHERS, INC.
195 McGregor St, Manchester NH 03102-3748 USA

*Classics in Modern Social Thought*